Rutland

Village by Village

Bob Trubshaw

Heart of Albion Press

Rutland Village by Village

Bob Trubshaw

Cover photograph of Thistleton church by Bob Trubshaw

ISBN 1 872883 69 9

Heart of Albion Press
2 Cross Hill Close, Wymeswold
Loughborough, LE12 6UJ

albion@indigogroup.co.uk

Visit our Web site: www.hoap.co.uk

Printed in the UK by Booksprint

Contents:

Preface

'No other county in England surpasses Rutland for
unspoiled, quiet charm...'

The pioneer local historian W.G. Hoskins penned these words in
1949. Remarkably, over the intervening fifty years Rutland has
remained essentially unspoiled, making its 'quiet charm' even more
valuable. The biggest change since 1963 has been the loss of about
five percent of the county to Rutland Water. Important though
Rutland Water has become for water sports enthusiasts,
ornithologists, anglers and cyclists, this little county has much more
of interest. Miles and miles of quiet byways pass through attractive
scenery and villages consisting of stone-built houses that are
reminiscent of the Cotswolds. Every village is worth stopping at to
explore – this book provides a concise guide to the more important
and accessible features.

The emphasis of this book is on what can readily be seen by a
visitor today, rather than on what has been lost, or the 'social history'
of places. Harking back to the antiquarians of the eighteenth century,
I have incorporated a wide variety of obscure and little-known facets
to the villages' histories, together with the more significant aspects of
the archaeological evidence. The county's churches are all of
interest and many are of national significance.

Most of the places described in this guide are on, or visible from,
public rights of way. However please show full respect for private
property and always follow the Countryside Code. Above all, 'Leave
nothing but footprints and take nothing but photographs'.

Cross-references to places described elsewhere in the gazetteer
are shown in **bold**.

Finally, a point of pedantry. Many church guides refer to
'Norman architecture' as the style of building used in Britain between
about 1066 and 1180. However the British style is closely linked to
the same style elsewhere in Europe, where it started several centuries
earlier. Of course there was no Norman conquest elsewhere in
Europe so this pan-European style is known as the Romanesque,
reflecting its clear origins in the Roman style of construction and
decoration. Scholarly writing about British architecture has long
referred to the Norman style as the Romanesque, and I have used the
term Romanesque throughout this guide. However many church
guide books retain the term Norman.

You will also need...

To navigate around Rutland the relevant Ordnance Survey 1:50,000 maps (numbers 130 and 141) are essential. Ordnance Survey grid references provided in this guide are for the church or (in the few cases where there is no church) the village centre. They are prefixed with the relevant OS map number (130 or 141). OS maps provide guidance on how to read grid references. However, if you are relatively new to looking up grid references, you may find remembering 'into the house before going up the stairs' is easier than the bland 'eastings before northings'.

While I fully appreciate the need to keep churches locked, I have nothing polite to say about the parishes where no information on current key holders is visible (and, in these days of mobile phones, key holders' phone numbers are much more helpful than addresses). If your interest in churches means you will want to attempt to see inside most of the churches in the county then I suggest you obtain a copy of the current Diocesan Directory from the Diocesan Office in Peterborough (phone number at time of going to print 01733 887000). This contains details of all clergy and churchwardens and is moderately priced.

Glossary

Art historians revel in creating 'typologies' and obscure terminology as a short-hand among themselves but which are more-or-less meaningless to the uninitiated. Sadly these terms are often used willy-nilly in church guide books by writers who, presumably seeking to impress others with their erudition, succeed instead in perplexing visitors. In case you come across them, here is a summary of the frequently used terms used to refer to the succession of different decorative styles.

Anglo-Saxon	600–1066
Romanesque (Norman)	1066–1180
Transitional	1175–1200
Early English (Gothic)	1190–1250
Geometric (Gothic)	1250–1290
Decorated (Gothic)	1290–1350
Perpendicular (Gothic)	1325–1530
Tudor	1485–1603
Baroque	C17–18
Queen Anne	early C18
Georgian (Neoclassical)	1714–1830
Gothic Revival	C19
Arts and Crafts	1860s to early C20

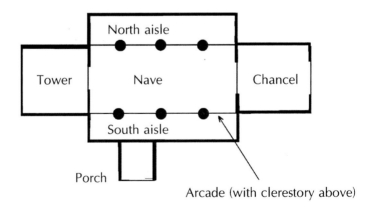

Schematic plan of a typical Rutland church. See Glossary for a more detailed explanation of terms used.

aisle: used here not to refer to the central walkway in the **nave** but to the extensions on the north and/or south sides of the nave, separated by **arcades**.

arcade: A series of arches on columns or piers, usually between the **nave** and the **aisles**.

aumbry: a small cupboard built into the wall of the chancel for storing the chalice and other liturgical vessels.

bellcote: An open structure on which the bells are hung, sometimes known as a bell turret. Twin bellcotes are especially common on Rutland churches.

box pew: Enclosed seating, often with doors, usually dating from the seventeenth or eighteenth century. They often were reserved for the use of specific families. Victorian church restorers were keen to remove these and replace them with 'open' pews.

broach: an octagonal spire merged into a square tower with triangular 'facets'.

capitals: the large blocks on top of a column or pillar, directly beneath the arch. They are often decorated, sometimes with stylised foliage, occasionally with figures or other more elaborated motifs.

chancel: the eastern part of a church, otherwise known as the choir.

clerestory: windows high up in the nave. They are often more recent than the rest of the nave, becoming very fashionable in the fifteenth century.

corbels: blocks of masonry partially set into walls and originally supporting roof timbers (although many are now functionless if the roof height has been raised).

crockets: rows of hook-like or leaf-like projections, usually on the edges of a spire.

foliate face: a face surrounded by leaves, or where the features are formed from leaves.

frieze:. Fairly self-explanatory - a continuous band of decorative carving with, usually, rather small figures of faces, animals or vegetation. One distinctive style of flower is very stylised and known as ball flower.

gargoyle: To be found on the outside of churches, around the tower and along the nave and aisle roofs. 'Gargoyle' is a term often used indiscriminately for any grotesque carving; I use it in its strict sense of a carving designed to drain rain-water off the roof away from the walls. (The word 'gargoyle' derives from the Old French word *gargouille* meaning 'throat'; the word 'gargle' shares the same origin.)

green man: a foliate face where branches sprout from the mouth, nose or eyes.

girning or **gurning:** pulling a face by putting one or both hands in the mouth.

hagioscope – see 'squint'

ha-ha: a wall above a ditch, preventing animals entering a park or garden without interrupting the view when seen from the house.

hatchment: a coat of arms hung in the church after a person's death.

label stop: the technical term for where the arch of a window or doorway meets the vertical sides.

lucarne: a narrow opening with a dormer-like gabled top, usually in a spire.

mass dial – see 'scratch dial'

nave: the part of the church where the congregation sit.

pilaster: a rectangular column projecting from a wall.

piscina: washing basin for the chalice and other sacred vessels, often richly carved.

reredos: an ornamental screen covering the wall behind an altar.

roof bosses: decorative carving along the centre of a roof.

rood loft: a 'platform' above the rood screen separating the nave and chancel. In medieval times this platform would have supported sculptures of the 'rood' i.e. Jesus on the cross, together with sculptures of the Virgin Mary and St John the Baptist. Almost without exception the rood lofts have gone, leaving only a set of twisting stairs that once provided access.

rood screen: a carved screen separating the nave and chancel.

scratch dial: Simple sundials to assist the clergy to assess the time of the Offices of the liturgy were apparently once common on the south side of churches. These are known as either 'scratch dials' or 'mass dials'. Unfortunately, both these names are misleading – the carving (at least on those that have survived!) is much deeper than a mere 'scratch'. But 'mass dial' is even more misleading as Mass was celebrated rarely before the mid-nineteenth century (perhaps only once or twice a year); the daily and weekly liturgy revolved around the Offices (such as matins and vespers). For lack of a better alternative, I refer to them as scratch dials.

Typically scratch dials are situated on the wall near to where the priest entered, so sometimes they are by the south porch; where there is a priest's door direct into the chancel the scratch dial may be there instead. The lines radiate from a small hole (where a stick would have been inserted); curiously so lines radiate above as well as below the centre, although this is apparently redundant effort!

Where multiple scratch dials are found at the same church the radiating lines are usually differently spaced. They may be 'winter' and 'summer' alternatives, or simply reflect the changing preferences of successive clergy.

sedilia: seats built into the wall, often in the form of beautifully carved niches. Usually there are three, one each for the priest, deacon and sub-deacon who assisted with the liturgy. The three seats are often ranked, with the tallest nearest the altar.

squint: a hole or window through the masonry that enabled priests at side altars to see the main altar, so that key events of the Mass could be synchronised when celebrated simultaneously at the different altars. Also known as a hagioscope.

stoup: a stone basin for holy water.

tympanum: a carved semi-circular stone intended to fill the gap between the door lintel and the arch above.

Acknowledgements

The information in this book is the result of about sixteen years of research and thanks are due to the great many people who have helped me over the years. Collective thanks to the authors of the many church and village guide books whose work has made my task much easier. Thanks too to the key holders of the county's churches for their essential help.

Some people deserve special thanks. Jill Bourn for many helpful discussions about place-names and the Braunston carving. Richard Knox for providing invaluable assistance about the archaeology. The staff of the Record Office for Leicestershire, Leicester and Rutland for a consistently helpful and efficient service. My greatest thanks to Alistair Ward for his extensive comments and corrections.

Highlights from Rutland's past

Rutland is a triangle of generally undulating land with its apex to the south. The eastern part includes an outcrop of ironstone, used extensively for building and giving a distinctive character to villages in that area. The excellent limestone from **Ketton**'s quarries has been used locally and for many prestigious buildings, including the Tower of London, York Minster and Exeter cathedral.

In 2001 a small housing development at **Glaston** led to the discovery of a unique Upper Palaeolithic site dating to 30–35,000 years ago. It appears to be a hyena's den but includes stone tools, suggesting that prehistoric people sheltered there too. Previously a hand axe from **Essendine** was the only evidence from this era. A scatter of flints from **Ridlington** indicates Mesolithic settlement, and sporadic finds of flints reveal that Neolithic people were present in most parts of the county.

There is evidence for many Bronze Age barrows, which gave their name to **Barrowden**. There is an exceptional number on the county's boundaries, suggesting that the land formed a Bronze Age territorial unit. Several hoards of bronze items confirm that Rutland was extensively occupied at this time, although settlement sites have so far eluded archaeologists. In contrast, evidence of Iron Age houses has been revealed, notably in the Gwash valley during the construction of Rutland Water. Most parish boundaries ignore Roman roads, this suggests they predate the roads and are based on Iron Age land units (see also page 5).

The Roman Ermine Street (later the Great North Road and now the A1) slices through the north-east of Rutland. Another Roman road, now known as Sewstern Lane or The Drift, branches from Ermine Street in **Greetham** parish and heads for the border at **Thistleton**. This later became a drovers' route and has mostly remained as a trackway. Another Roman road led west from **Thistleton** to **Market Overton, Teigh** and **Whissendine** then on to the Fosse Way at Syston. In the far south of Rutland a branch from the Gartree Road heads east from Medbourne to **Caldecott**, then on over the Welland to join Ermine Street at Water Newton.

There was a Roman fort at **Great Casterton** which grew into an important Roman trading town, but subsequently the market moved to nearby Stamford (originally part of Rutland until becoming 'independent', probably in the early tenth century). The Romano-

British small town at **Thistleton** included a temple built on the site of a late Iron Age precursor. Various Roman villas are known, especially on the easily-worked soils to the north-east.

There are few place-names recalling pre-Anglo-Saxon settlement so presumably the Anglo-Saxon settlement was extensive. **Hambleton** was probably the home of local early Anglo-Saxon kings, such as Rota who gave his name to the county. Compared to adjoining areas there is a dearth of later Scandinavian place-names. **Normanton** and the Norwegian who gave his name to **Glaston** are chief exceptions.

The evidence for early Anglo-Saxons in Rutland mostly comes not from how they lived in their separate farmsteads but from how they were prepared for the after-life. Several major cemeteries of the fifth to seventh centuries were excavated prior to modern archaeological techniques but revealed a wealth of grave goods, including high-status jewellery and weapons. The pattern of nucleated villages and associated roads that still shape midland England was created by the Anglo-Saxons, probably in the eighth century. The names of these villages sometimes preserve the names of the people who were notable at the time. Otherwise these people are mostly 'lost' to us, as the evidence for later Anglo-Saxon life is now buried under our villages; the earliest villagers were also the earliest occupants of the churchyards.

In the early tenth century Rutland became the dower lands of the English queens, such as Edith, the wife of Edward the Confessor (reigned 1042–66), who is commemorated by **Edith Weston**. On Edith's death in 1075 William the Conqueror retained Rutland for himself and converted a large part into a hunting forest.

Early in the twelfth century King Henry I created a royal forest in the northern and western parts of the county, known as the Rutland Forest. About a hundred years later only about one-third of this area was still royal forest; by the end of the fifteenth century it had shrunk further and was known as Leighfield Forest. The extent of this forest was steadily reduced until by about 1630 only about one square mile to the north of **Belton** remained.

Market Overton, as the name implies, was an important market starting in Anglo-Saxon times (although extensive finds of Roman coins suggest a possible earlier origin). However **Oakham** gradually become more important that Market Overton. Oakham market may have started in the early eleventh century, probably associated with a defensive site which, by the late twelfth century, had been replaced by a fortified manor house (which has survived as the 'castle'). This acquired stone defensive walls (since demolished) and a more castle-like setting in the thirteenth century.

The evidence of Norman church building is extensive. **Morcott** is the most complete example in the county, and there are interesting survivals at **Egleton** and **Stoke Dry**. **Tickencote** retains much Norman work although the present structure is the result of major restoration in the eighteenth century. **Brooke** church has a Romanesque font and masonry dating to the Roman era, although its main interest is the interior which has remained unchanged since the sixteenth century.

The turf maze at **Wing** is one of only eight in the country and was probably first cut in the medieval era.

The Bede House at **Lyddington** was built in the fifteenth century as a palace for the bishops of Lincoln. A splendid sixteenth century house at **Exton** is now ruinous although the church is worth visiting for its superb sepulchral effigies. A fine Palladian house was built at **Burley on the Hill** between 1694 and 1708. The village of **Normanton** was cleared in 1764 by Sir Gilbert Heathcote to build his Palladian house (it was demolished in 1925 and the site is now under Rutland Water). The unusual tower and portico of Normanton church date to 1826; it is now all but submerged by Rutland Water.

Teigh church has changed little since being rebuilt (apart from the thirteenth century tower) in 1782, and the interior retains the now-unusual configuration typical of those times.

As with elsewhere, enclosure of the fields started in the late eighteenth century and was mostly completed in the early decades of the nineteenth century. The addition of some fox coverts and the removal of a few hedges in the later twentieth century have done little to change the overall character of Rutland's fields over the subsequent two hundred years.

One of Rutland's claims to fame, fox hunting, started here in 1730. Around this time coaching inns were developing on the Great North Road, such as the famous Ram Jam Inn near **Stretton,** named after a potent drink sold to passengers as a winter warmer.

The Oakham Canal opened 1802, running from the River Wreake via Market Overton and Cottesmore, but had a short life because of poor water supply. The Welland Valley railway was built in the 1870s, including the magnificent viaduct near **Seaton**. However this did not lead to significant industrial development and the county has remained essentially rural.

Although **Uppingham** school had been founded in 1584 it remained small until after 1854, when the expansion of the school brought dramatic growth to the town. Almost all the buildings in the

Alexander's The Great Tower on the north shore of Rutland Water.

centre of Uppingham date to the nineteenth century or earlier, with many surviving from a substantial phase of rebuilding in the first half of the seventeenth century.

In 1977 3,100 acres of the Gwash valley (5 percent of county but some of its best agricultural land) were submerged to form Empingham Reservoir, now called **Rutland Water**. It is the largest manmade reservoir in Europe; previously there were only about 200 acres of water in the whole county. The shores are important for wintering wildfowl. Anglers catch about 50 tonnes a year of trout from the well-stocked waters, while dinghy sailors and wind surfers make full use of the surface.

Although 1960s and early 1970s housing developments have blighted some of the villages, the rot was curtailed more swiftly than in most rural areas and planners focused development on Oakham, Uppingham and a few larger villages. The population of the county grew from 20,000 in 1951 to 32,000 in 1981, mostly because of commuters from nearby large towns and cities. By 1991 the population had dropped slightly to 31,500.

This comparatively low population means that traffic is rarely a problem. Indeed, apart from pelican crossings and a bridge at Caldecott, the only set of traffic lights in Rutland is in Uppingham.

Origins of Rutland

Although well-known as England's smallest county, there is another fascinating aspect to Rutland's size – it is probably the only 'administrative unit' of land in use today in Britain that betrays its origins well over 2,000 years ago.

Being fairly practical folk, the Romans tended to respect existing territorial boundaries. Indeed they often took advantage of them by erecting small towns, forts or temples at places where two territories came together. There are two examples in Rutland, one on the west where the temple and small town near **Thistleton** straddles into Leicestershire, and one in the east where the fort, and later town, at **Great Casterton** marks the boundary with present-day Lincolnshire.

Beyond this little is certain about how the Roman boundaries correspond to the modern definition of Rutland. Still less is certain about the Iron Age boundaries which the Romans inherited. The best guess is that Rutland may have been one or two Roman *regiones*, perhaps based on **Hambleton**.

What we do know is that Rutland remained outside the English shire system that developed in the later Anglo-Saxon era. Uniquely, it retains the name of its early Anglo-Saxon king, Rota. Sadly, nothing is known of Rota. His name is typical of the early Anglo-Saxon period (late 6th and early 7th centuries). He does not appear in any written records, which also suggests he lived during the earlier phases of Saxon settlement.

Rutland is unique in England as the only large unit of land named after one person. This suggests Rota was renowned during his life for establishing control over this territory. Although we can only speculate about his exact status, he seems to have been a minor Middle-Anglian king.

Rota's land included Stamford, but probably not the more southerly and south-eastern parts of the later county (the part that was administered from Northampton in the eleventh century). Rota's Moor overlapped the later parishes of **Teigh** and **Whissendine** in the north-west of Rutland (these areas are still known as Rutmoor). His royal *tun* or settlement was probably **Hambleton.**

The almost complete absence of Scandinavian place-names is surprising because, from the ninth century, Rutland is in the very heart of the Danelaw. In contrast, most parts of both Leicestershire and Lincolnshire contain a high proportion of Scandinavian place-names. As Charles Phythian-Adams has noted, 'Rutland continues as a district which is distinguished by its extraordinary Englishness.'

By the mid-tenth century Rutland was part of the traditional dowry of the queens of England. The evidence suggests that this perpetrates a previous custom of Rutland being the dowry of the Mercian queens. Queen Edith, the occupant of the estates in 1066, was the latest in a long line of queenly predecessors, perhaps back as far as Alfred's sister Aethelswyth (who died in 888 and appears in historical records during the 860s).

Quite why Rota's name persisted and Rutland did not become 'Queensland' or other such name is now unknown. The logic of the English county system should have led to Rutland being combined with part of Lincolnshire to form 'Stamfordshire', but this too did not happen. Instead, for reasons that must have been unique to the locality, at some time before 1086 Stamford was detached from Rutland, which in turn led to **Oakham** developing as the administrative and market centre.

Even though the administration of Rutland was divided between Nottingham and Northampton during the eleventh century, the large royal hunting area that spanned this administrative boundary probably helped to keep the identity of Rutland.

All-in-all the survival of the territorial unit and its name makes Rutland even more of an oddity, and all the more interesting.

(This section is based on Charles Phythian-Adams 1977 and 1980; Cox 1994.)

Rutland village by village

Ashwell
130:866137
The eponymous well is situated on the edge of the village near a sharp bend on the **Oakham** road (130:874137). The neat structure has an inscription which reads:

> All ye who hither come to drink
> Rest not your thoughts below
> Look at that sacred sign and think
> Whence living waters flow

This is almost the same as the inscription on the well at **Greetham.**

In Water Lane are several attractive seventeenth century houses. St Mary's church is mostly fourteenth century with an earlier north

The holy well at Ashwell in 1988.

arcade which includes one arch of about 1200. It was thoroughly restored in 1851 by one of the leading architects of the Gothic revival, William Butterfield. The style of decoration was unprecedented in Rutland and must have created a very different impression from the Georgian interiors typical of churches at that time. The monuments include a wooden effigy of a knight (only one other wooden effigy has survived locally, at **Tickencote**) which dates to about 1320 and an incised marble effigy of the fifteenth century commemorating John and Rose Vernam. In the north chapel (now the vestry) is an alabaster effigy to John Vernam (son of the above) who was appointed Rector of Ashwell in 1465.

The churchyard cross and lych gate are also the work of Butterfield and date to 1851. In the churchyard is the gravestone of Rev James William Adams, the first clergyman to be awarded the Victoria Cross. This was for an act of bravery in December 1879, during the Afghan War.

Ayston

141:859009

This small ironstone-built village to the north of Uppingham is dominated by the early nineteenth century hall to the north of St Mary's church. The church has a thirteenth century nave. The north arcade is early thirteenth century and the south arcade followed about a hundred years later. The interior of the nave, with box pews, dates to about 1800. The tower and chancel are fourteenth or fifteenth century. A badly-eroded double thirteenth century effigy, fifteenth century stained glass of the Crucifixion and an eighteenth century font can be seen inside the church.

The area to the west of Ayston, towards **Belton** and **Wardley**, was a Norman hunting forest later known as Beaumont Chase. Previously this area was predominately woodland that included a pre-Christian sacred

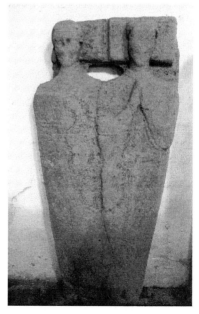

The double effigy at Ayston.

grove to Thunor (or Thor, the Scandinavian thunder god). Such groves are especially associated with ancient boundary areas, as is the case here. Evidence of another pre-Christian grove near an ancient boundary can be found about four miles to the south where there was a village called Holyoaks (141:844958), now just inside Leicestershire but historically in **Stoke Dry** parish.

To the south-west of the village is Castle Hill (141:894004). The remains of a substantial Norman motte survive with a large bailey to the east; the other sides are protected by steep slopes. This was probably the base for the foresters responsible for Beaumont Chase.

Barrow

130: 891152

This 'dead end' village is on the crest of a steep hill rising to about 460 feet (150 metres). On the crest is The Green where a prehistoric burial mound was once visible from lower in the valley. This tumulus or 'barrow' gave the village its name. On a smaller green stands the base and stump of an old market cross. About 150 yards to the east of the cross is a picturesque little thatched cottage. On one wall is a painted sign saying 'All Vagrants who are found Begging in this Town will be taken up & Prosecuted'.

The green and remains of the market cross at Barrow.

9

The remains of an old chapel of ease are in the garden of Church House. This chapel was replaced in 1831 by a small Gothic Revival church; this was pulled down in 1974.

Barrowden

141:945999

Prehistoric burial mounds on a hill also give Barrowden its name (from *beorg dun* – the hill with burial mounds on it). Archaeological and place-name evidence suggests that there was a number of burial mounds along the ridge towards **Seaton** and **Lyddington** overlooking the Welland valley and acting as 'boundary markers'.

St Peter's church is Romanesque in origin with rather curious proportions – the thirteenth century nave is wide but short. The tower and spire are fourteenth century. The strap hinges on the south door are believed to be late twelfth century; they are similar to those at **Brooke**. There is a monument to Rowland Durant who died in 1588. Old graffiti of shoes can be seen on top of the stone seats in the south porch. Pepperday Cottage, to the north of the church, is late seventeenth century.

A 'holy well cross' is mentioned about 1275 but neither well nor cross have survived. There is a fine fourteenth century bridge (later

Barrowden – one of the few village ponds in Rutland.

widened) over the River Welland on the road to Wakerley. There is a carved face above one arch.

The village green is overlooked by a number of attractive stone-built houses, including the late sixteenth or early seventeenth century Durant Farmhouse (with its wonderful example of 'polychrome' bands of ironstone and ironstone). To one side is the pond. The Baptist chapel at the east end of the green dates from 1819.

Belmesthorpe dovecote.

Belmesthorpe

130:043102

This small village to the southeast of **Ryhall** has a number of pleasing ironstone houses with roofs of Colleyweston stone. To the east of the village is a stone-built dovecote (130:045054).

Belton in Rutland

141:816014

This village added 'in Rutland' to its name in March 1982. There is a sixteenth century Tudor farmhouse. The Old Hall is early seventeenth century and Westbourne House is early eighteenth century in Queen Anne style. The older houses in the village are built of ironstone, some with roofs of Colleyweston stone. There are a number of Welsh slate roofs on the nineteenth century

One of the many gargoyles at Belton.

properties; although usually ubiquitous these are generally rare in Rutland.

St Peter's church stands on a mound. The building retains evidence of a fire in the thirteenth century. The font is also thirteenth century. An alabaster slab commemorates sixteenth century Haselwoods, who lived at the Old Hall. Look out for the drain in the south aisle piscina in the form of a monster's head. The church reveals several phases of building and alteration in the thirteenth and fourteenth centuries, and perhaps a little later. Much of the interior dates to 1897–1901. Outside there are lots of gargoyles on the south side and a tongue poker on a south aisle window. On top of the churchyard wall is a double partial effigy that has survived from the thirteenth century.

Bisbrooke

141:887996

Secreted among some of the narrowest lanes in Rutland is the village of Bisbrooke, with some fine examples of stone-built houses from the sixteenth to eighteenth centuries. St John the Baptist's church was rebuilt in 1871, although the tower (in the form of the double bellcote characteristic of Rutland) was not completed until 1914. In the south side of the churchyard is a limestone tombstone carved to depict a wagon drawn by four horses.

The wagon and horses tombstone at Bisbrooke.

Braunston

141:833066

This attractive village has a number of notable buildings. Quaintree Hall House has a Georgian front enclosing an older building, probably of the sixteenth century.

All Saints stands on a slight mound within the churchyard, which itself rises up from the east. There is an early thirteenth century Romanesque doorway, font and chancel arch. The rest of the building is mostly fifteenth century (although the apparently fourteenth century tower may have been rebuilt in the 1720s) and was restored between 1887–90. Inside look out for the traces of wall paintings (possibly fifteenth century) and tiny heads decorating the fourteenth century north aisle.

In the churchyard two slate tombstones, dated 1787 and 1795, depict the Resurrection. The most famous occupant of the churchyard, a carving of national importance, now stands to the west of the tower. About 1900 she was discovered face down being used as a doorstep. Although often referred to as a pagan goddess or 'Earth Mother' (or even as a 'sheela-na-gig', although she is not in the pose characteristic of such carvings) there is no evidence that she is pre-Christian.

Stylistically the carving has no near equivalents. Despite this, a number of writers consider that this carving may be Anglo-Saxon or, even more fancifully, Iron Age. Given that Braunston church is close to a boundary of Rutland that was disputed in Anglo-Saxon times (the nearby place-name Flitteris Wood derives from the Old English word *flitteris,* meaning 'a brushwood region of disputed ownership') this carving just possibly might have been an Anglo-Saxon boundary marker, perhaps parodying the Mercian queens who owned Rutland during the late ninth and tenth centuries. But by this time England was thoroughly Christianised, so although she may have been a rather scurrilous 'queen', she was never intended to be a goddess.

More realistically, the massive stone 'base' suggests she once stuck out horizontally, face down, from near the top of the tower. Such decorative figures are known as 'hunky punks' in Somerset, where they are known to date to the thirteenth and fourteenth centuries. The word 'punk' at this time had connotations of a whore; Quaintree Hall House nearby on the green takes its name from 'queen tree' and, again, until recent decades, the word 'queen' also had a double meaning as whore. If the carving is thirteenth or fourteenth century this would fit well with the probable date of the original tower. If the carving was originally situated on the tower then

The Braunston 'queen'.

it may well have been buried as a doorstep during the rebuilding of the 1720s. Unless further evidence comes to light there is no reason to suppose that this figure is earlier than the thirteenth century and may even be from the fourteenth century.

The roof of Quaintree Hall House has been dated by dendrochronology to 1295–1305. The stone walls date from the sixteenth century, replacing previous timber-framed construction, and may have been spoils from the demolition of **Brooke** Priory.

Brooke

141:850057

The only monastery in Rutland, an Augustinian priory owned by Kenilworth with only three canons, was founded here before 1153. Nothing of this priory survives above ground. In the sixteenth century Brooke Hall was built on the site but this building has also disappeared, apart from a ruined gateway and an octagonal porter's lodge, converted to a dovecote in the eighteenth century. Extensive earthworks of formal gardens, perhaps incorporating earlier earthworks from the priory, also survive. The red brick house now on the site, known as Brooke Priory, is seventeenth century. The Old Rectory opposite the church is probably the oldest surviving house in the village.

Interior of Brooke church.

St Peter's church is very attractively situated. It has a rather idiosyncratic thirteenth century tower that appears to taper outwards and Romanesque south doorway of about 1160, rebuilt at some time with a pointed apex. The north arcade is also Romanesque, dating from the mid-twelfth century, as is the square font decorated with arcading. The chancel, chapel, north aisle and south porch were all rebuilt in 1579, which is an unusual time for church building. The box pews and pulpit are also late sixteenth century. In the chapel there is a fine effigy depicting Charles Noel, who died aged only 28 in 1619.

Thankfully the restoration of 1878–9 made no changes to the interior, so the visitor to this church walks into a church that has changed little in over 400 years (although the seating in the north-east of the nave is probably a result of the nineteenth century restoration). No other church in the country has remained as such a 'time capsule' from the late sixteenth century. The lack of unnecessary ecclesiastical 'furnishings' adds to the simple grandeur of the building.

Look out for the medieval parish chest made from a solid log and the late twelfth century hinges of the north door that resemble fish bones or menacing centipedes (similar to those at **Barrowden**). The parish also owns a 'Judas bible'; so called because a misprint in St Matthew's Gospel substitutes 'Judas' for 'Jesus'.

Burley on the Hill
130:883103

The place name means 'a defended place in a clearing'. Possibly this was a 'garrison' constructed in the late eighth or early ninth centuries to help defend the royal centre at **Hambleton** in the event of Viking attacks.

The village was of substantial size until 1375 when it seems to have been almost entirely destroyed by fire. On the village green is a modest building, formerly the village smithy. It is supposedly the inspiration for Henry Longfellow's poem 'The Village Blacksmith'. In the 1920s the building also featured on advertisements for Cherry Blossom boot polish. It remained in use as a smithy until 1930.

Burley House (not to be confused with Burghley House at Stamford) was originally erected by George Villiers, 1st Duke of Buckingham, in the 1620s. Except for the stable blocks, this was burnt down in the Civil War. An entirely new house was constructed in the 1690s by Daniel Finch, 2nd Earl of Nottingham.

The house is famous for its Doric colonnade and in some respects is comparable to the better-known houses of Chatsworth and Petworth. It is often described as being in the Palladian style, but it anticipates this era of architecture by about twenty years. Finch appears to have been his own architect (taking advice from various notable professionals of the day, including Sir Christopher Wren) and was inspired by a visit to Rome where he saw St Peter's being constructed, and recently-built family houses at Ragley in

The 'Cherry Blossom' smithy at Burley.

Warwickshire and Lowther Castle, Westmorland. Although on an impressive scale, the detail has been described as 'restrained' or, less favourably, 'bleak'. Much of the interior was badly damaged by fire in 1908 but restored in the style of the late seventeenth century. Often overlooked by visitors to the main house is Home Farmhouse, which was designed by John Nash about 1795 as a pair of ornate cottages but later converted to one house and then further enlarged.

The formal gardens have been laid out three times, most recently in 1795. The walls around the park, formerly a medieval hunting park, are six miles long. The great avenue leading south was halved in length when Rutland Water was constructed

Holy Cross church was all but rebuilt during the restoration of 1869–70; the tower was restored in 1913. The north arcade dates from about 1180–90, and the south arcade is early thirteenth century. The font is fifteenth century. The clock is an important example of seventeenth century craftsmanship. Effigies of an unidentified fifteenth century knight and his wife are now near the tower arch. The white marble sculpture of a young woman commemorates Lady Charlotte Finch, who died in 1813.

In the churchyard is a gravestone depicted with mason's tools; there are curious carvings on the reverse of this and some other gravestones.

Caldecott

141:868937
The village takes its name
from a 'cold cottage' or
traveller's shelter. This may
have been the ruins of Roman
settlement surviving into
Anglo-Saxon times, as remains
have been found near the
church and also towards the
River Welland. A Roman road
crossed the Welland here on
its way from High Cross

Scratch dial, Caldecott church.

(straddling the Leicestershire and Warwickshire border on Watling
Street, now the A5) via Medbourne (Leicestershire) to Ermine Street
(later the Great North Road, now the A1) at Wansford
(Northamptonshire).

The village mostly comprises ironstone buildings, with bands of
limestone; some date from the sixteenth to eighteenth centuries. St
John the Evangelist's church incorporates Roman tiles in the walls.
There is also a 'scratch dial' or 'mass dial' (see Glossary). Inside, the
rather odd font dates to about 1300. Some traces of Romanesque
stonework survive, although most of the structure is thirteenth or
fourteenth century but was subjected to various restorations between
1862 and 1910. The spire had been rebuilt soon after 1797 when it
was 'shattered' by lightning.

Clipsham

130:970164
Pottery and late Roman military metalwork was found at the site of a
Roman villa in the parish.

Various limestone buildings, including two seventeenth century
farmhouses, make this a pleasing village. The local oolitic limestone
was quarried from the thirteenth century, although the stone is now
only extracted just over the Lincolnshire border.

Clipsham Hall is surrounded by a glorious yew hedge and
amazing topiary created in the 1880s by the Head Forester, Amos
Alexander but (as another guidebook politely puts it) 'much
simplified' by the Forestry Commission since the 1960s. Portraits of
the publican and policeman of the 1880s are among the losses.

The Clipsham yew tree avenue in 2002.

Access is from a car park about a mile to the north-east of the village (130:980169).

St Mary's church, near the Hall in the park to the north of the village, is bordered by lime trees. Inside is a Romanesque font and north arcade. The tower is late thirteenth or early fourteenth century, with a curiously-designed fourteenth century spire. Look out for the frieze of small human heads around the tower. The main restoration took place in 1858 although the high-quality oak seats and other woodwork date from the 1860s.

Cottesmore

130:903136

The prehistory of the village includes Bronze Age burials and Roman and Saxon remains. The 'Cottesmore hoard' of Bronze Age artefacts discovered in 1906 is on display in Rutland Museum, **Oakham.**

On the road to **Burley** is Alstoe Mount, a Norman motte and the remains of defensive ditches (130:894120). This site had previously been the meeting place for the 'hundred' or Anglo-Saxon local administration. Nearby are humps and bumps from the now-deserted village of Alsthorpe.

St Nicholas also has Norman origins, as is revealed by the Romanesque south doorway (now moved) and part of the exterior of

Alstoe Mount, the remains of a Norman motte.

the north wall. The tower, spire and chancel are thirteenth century and the rest of the church fourteenth/fifteenth century. The spire has unusually long apertures ('lucarnes'). The rather strange font has a bowl of the fourteenth or fifteenth centuries on a square base of about 1200. The present appearance of the church derives from a series of repairs and restorations undertaken between 1830 and 1867.

Two aspects of transport history overlap on the **Ashwell** side of the village. The remains of the Melton to Oakham canal (which had a very brief working life) run underneath a section of disused railway that is now home to the Rutland Railway Museum.

Cottesmore Airfield now dominates the area to the north-east of the village. It was built in 1935 and in recent years has been the base for Tornados.

Edith Weston

141:927054

The village takes its name from Eadgyd, queen of Edward the Confessor (c.1003–66). The 'west tun' is because it is west of the Anglo-Saxon royal manor of **Ketton**.

The so-called Domesday Oak can be seen from the path running along the shore of Rutland Water, in the garden of 'The Limes' to the north-east of the church, although it probably does not date back to

Edith Weston cross base.

1086. The base of a medieval cross survives in the centre of the village (141:927053). One of the oldest buildings in this attractive village is the Old Rectory, dated 1626. A subsequent rectory, an elegant stone building of about 1800, is now called Ladycroft.

St Mary's church still reveals much of its late twelfth century origins, including some decorative carving on capitals and elsewhere. Parts of the chancel arch also date to about 1170 although it was rebuilt in 1250. The north arcade was probably built 1190–5. The tower and graceful octagonal spire are fourteenth century, with bold bug-eyed gargoyles on the corners of the tower. In 1865 the chancel was rebuilt with an impressive vaulted roof. An old stone altar slab is now in the north aisle. The memorial to Sir Gilbert Heathcote (a founder of the Bank of England and Lord Mayor of London in 1711) was previously at **Normanton** and moved when the church was deconsecrated during the construction of Rutland Water. The turret clock made by John Watts in the late seventeenth century (but not as early as 1658, as often stated) is now in Rutland Museum, **Oakham**, and has been restored to working order. The churchyard contains some excellent seventeenth century box tombs.

Egleton

141:876075

Rutland has many outstanding churches and St Edmund's at Egleton is one of the gems. The exterior provides few clues as to the exceptional Romanesque interior, which is either late Saxon or early Norman, with clerestory windows added in the fourteenth century. It was originally constructed with side aisles but these were removed in the thirteenth century. Above the south doorway is a tympanum with geometrical figures, a winged 'dragon' and a lion. The shafts supporting the late Saxon or early Norman chancel arch are carved, and the thirteenth century font has wheel carvings.

Evidence of later eras can also be be seen. Part of an old rood screen which is now under the tower arch. A wall painting of the Royal Arms is above the chancel arch, and there are eighteenth century slate memorials in the chancel.

'Humps and bumps' to the east of the church betray the site of old cottages. There is an early dovecote, now adjoined to a modern building, at Home Farm (previously Manor Farm). At the east end of Main Street the road is truncated by Rutland Water; this is now the entrance to the nature reserve.

Egleton tympanum.

Empingham

141:950085

The Gwash valley to the west of the present village is now mostly submerged under Rutland Water but was the focus of considerable late Iron Age activity. The construction of Rutland Water revealed evidence of a Roman villa that may have been reused as an early Christian chapel in the seventh or eight centuries, as burials of this date just outside the building are aligned east-west. Two other Romano-British farmsteads dating to about the mid-second to mid-fourth centuries have been excavated to the west of the present village.

Evidence for extensive Anglo-Saxon settlement in the Gwash valley has been discovered plus various burials. These include a small late fifth to early seventh century cemetery discovered in 1967, and a larger cemetery of the same date excavated between 1974–5 in advance of the construction of Sykes Lane car park. The number of burials confirms that the area was quite densely settled at this time. Grave goods include amber beads, cowrie shells and ivory rings, showing that trading or social contacts extended as far as India or Africa.

Empingham continued to have a substantial population during the Middle Ages. When **Normanton** village was cleared in the eighteenth century, the villagers moved to Empingham.

At the side of the river (141:947083) is a broad moat over a metre in depth, with a causeway at the western corner. To the south are two fishponds. These are associated with the now-gone medieval manor house.

In 1470 an important battle during the Wars of the Roses took place north of the village. A local force led by Sir Robert Welles was routed by Yorkist forces under King Edward IV. It was known as the Battle of Losecoat Field, as the fleeing rebel leaders shed their identifying clothes. Bloody Oaks Wood near the A1 (130:970114) is near the site of the battlefield, presumably the scene of dramatic conflict. As a consequence of the fighting **Pickworth** village seems to have been destroyed.

St Peter's church is approached along an avenue of beech and sycamore trees; the church is surrounded by limes. The chancel and nave arcades are thirteenth century (unusually the south arcade is older than the north arcade); much of the rest is fourteenth century, including the impressive tower and steeple. This church escaped drastic restoration because there was one 'very conservative' vicar for most of the nineteenth century. The interior is largely thirteenth

Empingham dovecote.

century (including the attractive sedilia and piscina), with some fifteenth century changes. Remains of old wall paintings survive over the south door and in the south transept. Some original medieval glass survives in the upper parts of the east window of the north transept.

At the east end of the main street is a house called The Wilderness which is an example of plainer seventeenth century design. The three-arch bridge over the River Gwash to the south of the church is late seventeenth century. The front of Prebendal House, to the south-east of the church was built about 1700. A round stone dovecote now stands in a field to the north of the village (141:949089); inside is room for no less than 700 birds.

In 1980 a very modern monument appeared. Alexander's 9.3 metre high bronze sculpture called 'The Great Tower' was erected on the north shore of Rutland Water (see photograph on page 4). Sadly its sense of monumentality has been lost by the featureless landscaping and over-close proximity of scruffy woodland. The oh-so-seventies landscaping of Rutland Water has a pervasive alien quality that is reminiscent more of Milton Keynes than an otherwise unspoilt Midlands shire.

Essendine

130:049128

Aerial photography has revealed evidence for numerous ploughed-out prehistoric burial mounds to the north, east and south-east of the present village. The eastern parish boundary, also the county boundary, follows the line of a Bronze Age triple-ditch earthwork associated with a burial mound and three ring ditches (which probably once had burials at their centre too). This suggests that this part of the boundary of Rutland dates back over three thousand years.

Soon after the Conquest the Normans built an excellent chapel, now the parish church, at Essendine. The chancel arch and south doorway are probably mid-twelfth century. Above this is a tympanum depicting Christ in majesty with two angels, in a style that is more typical of France than England. The door jambs are also carved with such motifs as two men with crooks, a stag under a tree, and what may be intended to be Adam and Eve under a tree. These are very unusual in England but are akin to carvings at **Stoke Dry**.

Essendine tympanum.

The Normans also built a castle which was subsequently extensively 'remodelled', probably in the late thirteenth century. The moat survives to the north-east of the church; an Elizabethan house is known to have stood within the moat. The present church lies with a still-visible rectangular earthwork that links to the former castle site. At some time the thirteenth century parish church, which stood at the other end of the village, fell into disuse and the Norman chapel became the parish church.

The castle was strategically situated close to the West Glen River. The road is now carried over a three-arch seventeenth century bridge, spoilt in 1956 by a modern concrete upper structure.

Exton

130:920112

A document of 1185 refers to Exton Park as a wooded farm enclosed for hunting deer. Indeed, at 1,500 acres (600 hectares) Exton was once Rutland's largest park; the current park is still 1,000 acres (400 hectares).

The church, dedicated to SS Peter and Paul, is one of the finest in Rutland with an unusual spire on an octagonal base. It was much restored in the 1850s. Inside is a late fourteenth century font with prominent faces. But the real splendours of this church are nine superb effigies depicting members of the two most important dynasties in Rutland, the Harington and Noel families. These monuments are excellent examples of the evolving styles fashionable from the fourteenth to eighteenth centuries. Three are by the nationally-famous sculptors Grinling Gibbons (1648–1721) and Joseph Nollekens (1737–1823). Gibbons' twenty-two feet high memorial in black and white marble to Baptist Noel is an early example of depicting the deceased in Classical dress. This larger-than-life (in all senses) creation may hold the record for the largest number of figures on one sepulchral monument, as no less than twenty-five people are depicted, including all four of Baptist's wives. Another unforgettable effigy depicts Anne Bruce (died 1628) dressed in a shroud; at her feet is a pelican holding a serpent in its beak.

Now hidden by shrubs, just to the east of the church are the ruins of an early seventeenth century house, Old Hall, which burnt down in 1810. New Hall was built nearby in the Jacobean style in 1850 around an old farmhouse that had been extended in 1811. It includes a Roman Catholic chapel built in 1868–9 for the family's use. A straight mile of chestnuts, limes, ash, birch, beech and sycamore lead to the park. In the park are large ornamental lakes and

The lodge cottages and *stag-surmounted gate piers at Exton.*

various follies, including a summerhouse called 'Fort Henry' at the side of the lake, built in 1785–8 in a 'Gothick' style. The entrance to the park has gate piers surmounted by stags.

Much of the village almost certainly once stood around the church (lots of humps and bumps can be seen to the south and south-east of the church). These buildings were probably cleared away when Old Hall was built in the sixteenth century as they are not shown on an engraving of the village prepared about 1739. The present village centre is a sycamore-shaded green surrounded by attractive stone cottages, many with thatched roofs. The oldest is probably a farmhouse in Top Street dated 1701. Tudor Cottage, to the south-east of the green; was 'collaged' together in the nineteenth century from medieval fragments. Near the school there is a well called Hawkswell Spring with eight pillars and a stone roof.

Glaston

141:896005

Glaston can boast the oldest evidence for human activity in Rutland. In 2000 excavations ahead of house building revealed an Upper Palaeolithic site dated to 30–35,000 years ago which seems to have been a hyenas' den, although stone tools suggest that humans also sheltered there. At the time the area was steppe-like grassland where mammoths, rhinos, giant deer, reindeer, bison, horses and early humans all lived. The den was on top of a sandy ridge with good

Glaston pond.

views. Substantial 'rafts' of limestone provided shelter, and the unusual geological conditions allowed the bones in the den to be preserved. This site is so far unique in Britain as no other open-air Upper Palaeolithic site has been discovered.

A pre-Christian Anglo-Saxon cemetery was discovered in 1946 while will sand was being excavated opposite the church.

The place name derives from 'Glathr's settlement'. The name Glathr is Norwegian and the only Scandinavian personal name in a Rutland place-name, although Scandinavian personal names are especially common in adjoining counties.

St Andrew's church has a central tower of the twelfth century with a rather short broach spire. Inside are twelfth century Romanesque arcades, a thirteenth century sedilia and marble coffin, and a fourteenth century monument. The south windows seem to be fourteenth century and the tracery appears unsymmetrical, until the two windows are looked at as a pair.

Other buildings of interest include an early eighteenth century house with mullioned windows to the immediate west of the Monckton Arms. Ten years older, with a date stone of 1696, is Coppice Farmhouse, to the east of the church. The nineteenth century brick rectory, just to the south of the church, surrounds an earlier stone house. A rather magnificent stone-built house with an L-shaped frontage is to the east of the village by the main road.

The old pond in Spring Lane (141:898006) has had its ramp restored. This enabled carts to swell their wheel rims in hot weather to prevent the iron rims detaching.

Great Casterton

141:002088

In June 1968 clay extraction in the parish revealed the fossilised bones of a dinosaur that lived about 175 million years ago. Known as *Cetiosaurus*, it is one of the most complete sauropod dinosaurs recovered in Europe. The reconstructed skeleton is now on display at New Walk Museum, Leicester.

This settlement owes its origin to there being a convenient crossing of the River Gwash for the Roman Ermine Street, later the Great North Road, and now the A1. Soon after the Roman conquest in AD 43 a fort, tucked into a large loop of the river, was constructed to guard the crossing. This was followed by a settlement developing to the east, which by AD 80 had acquired its own defences (unusually for Roman small towns in this region) and the fort was then abandoned. This town seems to have been involved in pottery production and iron working.

Substantial sections of the massive defensive ditches of the Roman town can still be seen to the north-east of the present village,

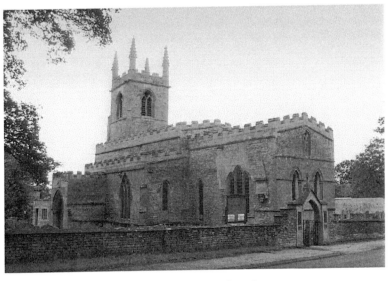

Great Casterton church.

29

parallel to the present day road to **Ryhall**. The whole fort covered an area of 18 acres (7 hectares); it is the only Roman site in Rutland that was primarily military.

Further to the north-east was a fourth century villa. Nothing is now visible above ground but the finds are in Rutland Museum, **Oakham**. The Roman cemetery was to the north of the defences, where the primary school now stands. By the fifth century Anglo-Saxons were buried alongside Romans, suggesting that mercenary troops brought from Germany had perhaps settled here (see also **Clipsham**). There is every reason to suppose that there has been a settlement here continuously since the Roman Conquest.

In either the late Saxon or early Norman era stone from the Roman ruins was reused to build a church, situated at the southern edge of the Roman town on the site of a *mansio*, a government-run 'inn', which had a bath house. The font dates from the Romanesque period although the present building is mostly-unrestored thirteenth century; note the attractive round-headed arcades. The effigies of three thirteenth century priests survive, two inside and one outside. The early clerestory with its circular windows is late thirteenth century. The fourteenth century tower is apparently the most recent phase of building. Of the same century is the ironwork on the south door. In the eighteenth century a pulpit with a sounding board or 'tester' was added, along with the arms of King George II in the tower arch.

In the churchyard are many interesting gravestones, including a slate with a rare depiction of the Resurrection; also look out for one showing the sacrifice of Isaac.

The trading activities at Great Casterton shifted in the early Anglo-Saxon era along the road to Stamford, probably because the River Welland was then navigable for small cargo-carrying vessels. With the Danish conquest of this region Stamford became the regional market town and continued to gain in importance, while the status of Great Casterton diminished.

In the medieval era a prominent ridge-top to the north (141:997116) was fortified. This was known as Woodhead Castle and the earthworks of the castle still abut an area of wood on the top of the ridge. The castle was ruinous by 1543.

Greetham

130:924146

The Roman Ermine Street slices through the north-east of Rutland. In the eastern part of Greetham parish Sewstern Lane (sometimes known as The Drift) branches from Ermine Street, going to **Thistleton** and on to form the Leicestershire–Lincoln-shire border. Sewstern Lane was used by the Romans but may be a prehistoric track.

Ironstone quarries and limekilns near the village seem to have been worked intermittently from Roman times to the nineteenth century.

Part of an Anglo-Saxon cross has been incorporated into the inside west wall of the south aisle of St Mary's church. Alongside are also Romanesque carvings including fragments of a twelfth century tympanum. The font is also Romanesque, dating from about 1200, and has four wonderful heads on the 'corners'. One depicts a

Greetham well head.

human with a very elongated tongue, two are animal heads and the fourth seems to be an imaginary 'beastie'. On the outside of the church are several dozen small heads around the nave and tower roof, they also include rather 'demonic' figures and probably date to the first half of the fourteenth century.

There is a sheep dip in the stream in the middle of a village street. Also in the village is a well head – perhaps in reality more of a 'conduit head' or even 'cistern head' (130:925145). Although the overall design is quite different to the better known well at **Ashwell**, the inscription is almost identical:

All ye who hither come to drink
Rest not your thoughts below
Remember Jacob's Well and think
Whence living waters flow

One of the most singular curiosities of the village is Halliday's workshop in Great Lane. Various fragments of ecclesiastical masonry are incorporated into the walls. William Halliday was responsible for repairing several Rutland churches (including **Exton**) in the nineteenth century and seems to have been fond of taking away old decorated stonework to incorporate in his own house. Interestingly, not all the stone looks so badly worn that it needed replacement...

Hambleton

141:900076

Before the flooding of Rutland Water there were three villages, Upper, Middle and Nether Hambleton. Old Hall, built 1610 (140:899070), is all that survives of Middle Hambleton; otherwise only Upper Hambleton remains above the shore line.

Hambleton was probably the power base for early Anglo-Saxon rulers of the region (such as Rota, who gave his name to Rutland) perhaps because of the dramatic hilltop location above the Gwash valley. Indeed, there has been speculation that Hambleton was the centre of a Roman *regio* or administrative district which, in turn, suggests that the place would have been important in the Iron Age. At some time, probably the late eighth or early ninth centuries, a more defended site or a garrison was built to the north at **Burley** as the name means the *burg* (defended place) in the clearing.

The former Post Office, Hambleton.

There was a weekly market and an annual fair at Hambleton throughout the Middle Ages and quite probably these date back to at least the Anglo-Saxon period.

St Andrew's church has traces of its Anglo-Saxon origins, although the building mostly dates from about 1180–90, with early thirteenth century arcades and various modifications in the late thirteenth century. The building was well-restored in the nineteenth century. Look out for the interesting Romanesque doorway and fourteenth century font. The thirteenth century tower is surmounted by a low broach spire of about 1230.

A late sixteenth century priest's house survives, much

restored, to the south of the church. Hambleton Old Hall dates to the early seventeenth century but has been subjected to various alterations. This should not be confused with Hambleton Hall, built in 1881 in the mock-rural style that was then fashionable, especially in the Home Counties. Near the church are several estate worker's cottages built in 1892 in an Art Nouveau style; one of these retains the stylish decorative metalwork from when it was the Post Office.

From the Hambleton peninsula there is a dramatic view over Rutland Water to Burley House in the north.

Ketton
141:982043
Aerial photographs have revealed extensive 'crop marks' of prehistoric settlements that have been ploughed away. In recent years archaeological excavations ahead of quarrying have revealed Roman burials and occupation sites, and a late eleventh century Anglo-Saxon village with a timber-built church.

One of the elaborately carved tombstones in Ketton churchyard.

Ketton has long been famous for its building stone. This particular type of oolitic limestone is fine-grained and has long been regarded as the perfect stone for delicate decorative carving, It has the advantage of being comparatively soft when quarried but hardens after exposure to air. The ability to ship the stone along the River Welland reduced the costs of transport and also explains why it is used more in Cambridgeshire than in places west of Ketton. Famous buildings built at least in part with Ketton stone include the Tower of London, York Minster, Exeter Cathedral, sculpture for Beverley Minster, several Cambridge colleges, Fleet Street law courts, Burley on the Hill house, various Norfolk and Suffolk churches, and many local churches. Since 1928 Ketton stone has been quarried only for cement manufacture.

St Mary's church has a fragment of an Anglo-Saxon cross. The oldest parts of the structure are the Romanesque west front and doorway. The tower is late twelfth century with a splendid fourteenth century spire, which probably took about 50 years to complete. The building was well restored in 1861 by one of the leading architects of the Gothic revival, Sir Gilbert Scott, (who was also responsible for St Pancras station, the Albert Memorial and numerous churches) although the chancel was restored by a different architect in 1863.

Curiously Ketton's church is not built from locally-quarried stone, but uses the shellier limestone from Barnack. However Ketton stone is used for the exuberantly-decorated eighteenth century gravestones in the churchyard. Many of these were carved by members of the Hibbins family and the memorial to William Hibbins (near the lych gate) is decorated with mason's tools. At the crossroads at the south end of the village the Hibbins built a house in 1890 that is decorated with exceedingly eclectic examples of the masons' art – including gargoyles. The war memorial in the churchyard was erected in 1921. Just to add further geological variety, this is carved in Clipsham stone, which has the best resistance to weathering of all the oolitic limestones quarried for buildings.

The older houses of the village use local stone, including Colleyweston 'slates' for the roofs. They make Ketton one of the more remarkable of the many attractive stone-built villages in Rutland. To the east of the church is a triple-arch bridge which is seventeenth century, although inevitably 'restored' over the years. To the south of the church is a house known as The Priory (although it was never a priory but rather a prebendal manor house which has been privately-owned since 1723); the oldest part is dated 1618 although there have been several phases of additions in the seventeenth, eighteenth and nineteenth centuries. In the eastern part of its grounds is a sizable dovecote.

The tower of a windmill survives on the lane to **Edith Weston** (141:972046). At the opposite end of the village, by the railway crossing over the **Cottesmore** road, are mid-nineteenth century buildings including former maltings, gasworks and a hotel.

Langham

130:844113

There are prehistoric earthworks on Ranksborough Hill (130:823116) which may be the remains of an Iron Age settlement. A bronze Roman figurine was found nearby in the late nineteenth century which is now on display in the British Museum. Since the 1980s the site has been a caravan site and squash courts.

SS Peter and Paul's church is situated in the loop of a stream. The tower is thirteenth century, the tall spire and arcades fourteenth century, the font, roof and magnificent window in the south transept are fifteenth century. The fourteenth century clerestory is unusual as it continues over the chancel arch.

The village is rather long and scattered. The most interesting old houses are in Church Street. The Old Hall, next to the church, was built in 1665; the west wing was added in 1926.

Commercial brewing was started at Langham in 1858 by a local farmer, Richard Westbrook Baker. The business had several

The Roman figurine of Jupiter from Ranksborough Hill.
© The British Museum

owners in subsequent decades. In 1896 George Ruddle became the brewing manager and, on the death of the previous owner, bought the business in 1911. Even though he died in 1923, the brewery retained the name Ruddle's. Their 'County' brand enjoyed considerable success in the late 1970s and early 1980s but after 1986 various changes of ownership were accompanied by a decline in sales. The brewery was closed in 1999, and Ruddles beer is now brewed in Bury St Edmunds.

Little Casterton
141:018099

A medieval gatehouse survives at Tolethorpe Hall, on the road to **Ryhall**. The main building is a sixteenth century manor house with eighteenth century additions although little of historical interest has survived inside. The grounds are locally famous for the open air theatre. To the west of the hall is a stone-built watermill with unusual cast-iron windows.

All Saints church, by the River Gwash, is somewhat remote from the village. There is a Romanesque tympanum on the inside wall of the aisle. This is decorated with a Tree of Life and two triple rosettes that are said to denote the wheel of eternity. Until 1908 this stone was used face down as the sill of the west window. The north arcade and north doorway are about 1200 and are probably contemporary

Little Casterton tympanum.

with the tympanum, which presumably was originally placed over the south door. The remainder of the building is thirteenth century, apart from the clerestory of a century or two later, although the chancel was rebuilt in accurate thirteenth century style during the 1830s (one of the first major restorations in Rutland). The interior furnishings were mostly replaced between 1906–8. There are some rare late thirteenth century paintings on the wall around the west window. The fourteenth century piscina canopy is decorated with human heads. The flower-shaped drain in the floor is said to have come from **Pickworth** church. Some of the painted glass in the south windows of the chancel are also fourteenth century. Of a similar date is the fine memorial brass to Thomas Burton, who died in 1381, and his wife. The lower half of the chancel screen is sixteenth century.

Lyddington
141:877970

Lyddington has a long, very attractive main street of houses built from local ironstone. Many of these are seventeenth and eighteenth century, such as the priest's house of 1626 to the south of St Andrew's church.

The only property in Rutland in the guardianship of English Heritage is the Bede House. This was built in the fifteenth century (probably between 1436 and 1449 by Bishop Alnwick) as an opulent manor house – sometimes grandly termed a palace. A substantial property existed here earlier, as a filled-in moat that may be twelfth century has been discovered, and permission to build defences here was granted by the king in 1336. What has survived is only part of the original complex, perhaps just the southern part of a much larger arrangement around a courtyard. The construction is local limestone with Collyweston 'slates'. Painted glass from the mid- and late-fourteenth century survives.

After the Reformation the house was owned by, among others, Lord Cromwell and William Cecil (Lord Burghley). In 1602 William Cecil's son, Thomas, converted the building to an almshouse for twelve poor men and two women. It is the 'bede house' because those who lived there were expected to pray ('biddan') for their benefactor. It remained in this use until the twentieth century. For no less than twenty years between 1945 and 1965 the Ministry of Works undertook a lengthy restoration. Also of interest is the octagonal turret with a footpath through it between the Bede House and the church. This was built as a gazebo to look over the medieval formal gardens by Bishop Smith between 1496–1514. About 200 metres to

The foliate face inside Lyddington church erected in 1991.

the north-east of the churchyard the now-dry bishops' fishponds can be discerned.

St Andrew's church is unusual as it is aligned from north-east to south-west. The tower and chancel are 1320–40; earthenware jars high up in the walls of the chancel are an early experiment in acoustics. The rest of the building is fifteenth century, apart from the vestry of 1849. Two coffin lids of the thirteenth or fourteenth century now stand under the tower. The memorial brass to Edward Watson (died 1520) was rather 'new fangled' in its day as the inscription is in 'modern' Roman lettering rather than the 'Black Letter' script typical of the time. The remains of wall paintings are fifteenth century but they defaced were during the Reformation. In the north aisle windows the tops of windows include original fifteenth century glass depicting human faces.

The unusual, perhaps unique, 'wrap around' communion rails were installed in 1635 and represent a compromise between those who thought the 'altar' should be in its traditional position at the east end of the church and the more radical protestant ideas of the time who argued that the 'communion table' should be near the middle of the church.

The aisles and nave are populated with numerous animal and human grotesques. These are presumably fifteenth century, apart from the pair facing each other at the chancel end of the nave, a foliate face and portrait of the Bishop of Peterborough, which were carved in 1991. On the exterior of the tower look for 'face pulling' (or 'girning') gargoyles.

The stump and base of a medieval cross were re-erected on the village green in 1930. Honeypot Spring survives only as a street name.

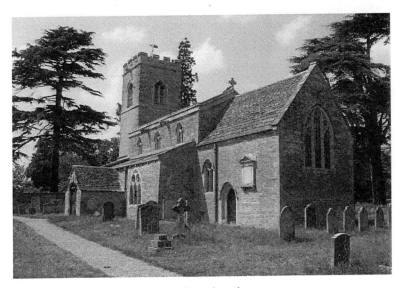

Lyndon church.

Lyndon

141:907044

Lyndon Hall was built between 1671–3 to the west of the village. As with **Burley** House, the owner learnt sufficient about architecture to design the building for himself, although changes were made in the nineteenth century, such as moving the entrance to the north. The stables, partly seventeenth century, are surmounted by a stone cupola and a weathervane in the form of a stag. Gilbert White, the Selbourne naturalist, stayed here often. His sister was married to Thomas Barker of Lyndon, one of the first meteorologists. Top Hall, to the north on a hill, is of a similar date.

St Martin's church is fourteenth century (restored rather heavy-handedly in 1866) although inside is a strange twelfth century Romanesque font decorated with crude serpentine carvings. It was discovered in the churchyard during the 1866 restorations. These restorations are responsible for the alabaster reredos and rather over-imposing pulpit. Look out for the rood loft stairs, a three-eyed face on the south porch doorway and some miserable-looking faces decorating the nave arcade. Outside there are interesting gargoyles.

Manton

141:881047

Manton is one of the few villages in the country with a railway tunnel running underneath. This does not detract from the generally very pleasing streetscapes of houses, many of which date from the seventeenth and eighteenth centuries.

The Romanesque tower of St Mary's church is topped by a rather massive thirteenth century bellcote and west front. The aisle arcades and north doorway were constructed about 1200. The rest of the church was mostly rebuilt in the fourteenth century. The chancel was rebuilt in 1796 with large Georgian windows. The font is Romanesque. Probably thirteenth or fourteenth century is the stone coffin decorated with a beautiful cross. Also notable is the tall almsbox which is of 1637. Rather unusual is the memorial to Robert Heathcote, who died in 1917, as this has a low-relief portrait of the deceased.

The churchyard is one of the most attractively kept in the county. Among the many gravestones look out for one decorated with what at first glance might be taken for a pair of mermaids. They are more accurately 'Belvoir angels' – an eighteenth century motif of a face

The Manton 'mermaids'.

with two wings intended to depict the soul of the deceased – although these have exceptionally extensive scroll decoration.

Market Overton

130:885165

Market Overton has a long history. A Roman pottery kiln was discovered in a field just to the north. Nearby was an Anglo-Saxon cemetery. One of the finds was a unique Anglo-Saxon water clock made of very thin bronze which took just over an hour to sink when placed in water. Burials at two other Anglo-Saxon cemeteries to the east of the village were accompanied by high status gold and silver ornaments.

A market is first documented in 1200. The original site may have been on or near the Roman temple on the parish boundary with **Thistleton**. Later the market was held in the field to the east of the church.

The tower arch inside the church of SS Peter and Paul contains the best example of Anglo-Saxon architecture in the county. Two substantial fragments of Anglo-Saxon cross shafts are built into the outside of the base of the tower. The stile in the north-west side of the churchyard wall incorporates columns that are either reused Roman or Anglo-Saxon masonry. The font base is an early thirteenth century capital upturned; the font itself is made from a reused twelfth century

The largest of the three Anglo-Saxon cross shaft fragments now incorporated into the base of the church tower.

41

capital. Be sure to take note of the early fourteenth century church door and ironwork. The nave is later fourteenth century and the exterior of the church looks almost entirely fourteenth century.

The churchyard sundial was reputedly donated by Sir Isaac Newton (his mother or grandmother was from Market Overton). The stocks and whipping post on the village green are overlooked from a nearby building by the head of Sir Isaac Newton. The village contains many attractive stone houses with a mix of thatched and stone roofs.

Although the species is now rare in Rutland, two elm trees flank the bus shelter to the east of the churchyard.

Along the road to **Teigh** is the wharf of the disused Oakham Canal, with stone- and brick-built warehouses (now houses).

Morcott
141:924007

This village has many good stone-built houses, suggesting wealthy inhabitants in the seventeenth and eighteenth centuries. Older houses include the Old Parsonage (now known as Sundial House), built in 1627 on the north-east of the church, which has most attractive alternative bands of ironstone and limestone. On the other side of the church is the Tudor-style Rectory/Hall built in 1830, next to the Manor House of 1687.

A man's head with stylised fir cones. One of the wonderful Romanesque corbels inside Morcott church.

St Mary's church is one of Rutland's gems. The arcade, south door and lower parts of tower are all Romanesque, making this the most complete church in the county built by the Normans. There are wonderful animals on the capitals of the arcade and ambitious serpents around the capitals of the tower arch.

In the west wall of the tower a fourteenth century doorway and window have been inserted. The circular window above these may be Romanesque. Although the chancel was rebuilt in the fifteenth century the thirteenth century chancel arch was retained along with a fourteenth century tomb. The beautifully carved pulpit is seventeenth century.

The 1732 Baptist chapel is early but the building was heavily restored in 1903. On the **Barrowden** road the village windmill was restored in 1968 from a two-storey stump to a four-storey house complete with ogee cap, sails and fantail.

Normanton
141:933064
The place-name derives from 'the settlement of the Norwegians'. Compared to adjoining counties there is a dearth of Scandinavian place-names in Rutland. Normanton and the Norwegian who gave his name to **Glaston** are the chief exceptions.

Neo-Classicism loses out to twentieth century materialism at Normanton.

For various reasons the history of Normanton is mostly about what has gone. The village was demolished in 1764 by Sir Gilbert Heathcote to improve the park of his magnificent Palladian-style house (the site of the cleared village is now flooded by Rutland Water). Along with **Exton** and **Burley**, Normanton was one of the three great estates in Rutland. Heathcote's house was itself demolished in 1925, although the stable block, clock tower and part of the garden remain on the shore of Rutland Water.

In 1764 Heathcote also demolished the fourteenth century church, apart from the tower which survived until 1826 when it was replaced with a tower and portico based on St John's church in Smith Square, London. The chancel and nave were again rebuilt in 1911 to match the tower. When Rutland Water was created the sepulchral monuments were transferred to **Edith Weston** church. The building was deconsecrated and half-submerged. It is now a museum about water supply. Its curious location projecting from the shore makes it one of the best-known landmarks on Rutland Water. Close up, the concrete and rubble 'defences' detract greatly from the elegance of what is otherwise the best example of Neo-classical elegance in Rutland.

Nearby Normanton Park Hotel has one of Britain's oldest cedar trees.

North Luffenham
141:934033
The village is situated on a probable Roman road running south from **Empingham** (part of this survives to the east of **Normanton** but most has been lost to **Cottesmore** airfield). A large sixth and seventh century pagan Anglo-Saxon cemetery was discovered to the north of the village. A surprisingly high number of the men were buried with swords, suggesting that they may have been an elite body guard associated with the royal centre at **Hambleton.**

St John the Baptist's church retains much of its late thirteenth and early fourteenth century origins, although it was heavily restored between 1870–5 leaving the interior rather unattractive. The north arcade is late twelfth century and the south arcade followed a few decades later. There are traces of thirteenth century wall paintings and much fourteenth century glass in the chancel windows. The nave roof is fifteenth century and the multitude of angels and bosses retain their original colour. The impressive sedilia is also fifteenth century. The pulpit is sixteenth century. There are monuments to members of the Digby family and a portrait bust of Susanna Noel, who died in

1640. The nave roof is supported by figurative corbels and wooden angels. Some lively faces decorate the arches on the south side of the nave.

One of the enigmatic faces dating from the 1870s restoration of North Luffenham church.

In a small wood on the crest of a ridge on the parish boundary with **Morcott** (141:928023) is an artificial mound about 2 to 3 metres high. Various explanations have been offered, from an Anglo-Saxon burial mound, a small Norman castle, to a gun emplacement for the Civil War siege of North Luffenham Hall. Most probably it is a 'prospect mound' created in the seventeenth century to provide a vantage point for looking at the park.

North Luffenham Hall (until 1806 known as Digby House) is a sixteenth century manor house with a timber-framed tithe barn dated 1555 adjacent. It was extended in 1910–11. To the south-west of the church is a large semi-circular ha-ha (see Glossary), built in the middle of the eighteenth century as part of the gardens of Luffenham House, which was demolished in 1806. Probably also part of these gardens are moat-like earthworks (141:928032 and 935028) that may have been ornamental fishponds.

A house known as 'Pastures House', on the road to **Morcott,** was built in 1901 and is an example of the work of the nationally-important architect and designer Charles Voysey (1857–1941). His houses were characteristically asymmetrical with massive supporting walls, rough-cast walls and long sloping roofs.

Oakham

141:861089

Oakham is the county town of Rutland. The oldest evidence of settlement here is the foundations of an Anglo-Saxon building discovered in the early 1990s ahead of building work in South Street. The so-called castle (more a fortified manor house) was built about

The oldest surviving English castle hall at Oakham.

1180 and is the earliest surviving hall of any English castle. The capitals may have been carved by the same masons who worked on Canterbury Cathedral. There is copious use of dog-tooth decoration. The figures on the ends of the gables outside are rare survivals from this era; they are said to depict a centaur and Samson with a lion. The castle owes its survival, as does a similar Norman great hall in Leicester, to its long-standing use as a court of law. Assizes were held here from 1229 until 1970 and it remains in use as a magistrates' court. The unique custom of every peer passing through the town being required to forfeit a horseshoe may have something to do with William de Ferrers ('farriers') being the person who built the hall, although there is no record of the custom before the fifteenth century.

The banks of the bailey still survive as the castle boundaries (the stone walls are probably no older than the thirteenth century). A motte once stood in the south-east corner of the bailey but has mostly been removed.

All Saints's church is essentially fourteenth century but underwent a radical restoration by one of the leading Victorian 'Gothic revivalists', Sir Gilbert Scott, between 1857–9, whose main change was to build the east window of the chancel in the 'Decorated' style of about 1300, whereas the rest of the building is in the more severe 'Perpendicular' style of the later fourteenth century. Unusually the early thirteenth century south doorway and late thirteenth century porch are seemingly the oldest surviving parts of the structure. The font is early thirteenth century and would have originally been supported on eight columns. It is now supported by what may have been either a Romanesque capital or the base of a fourteenth century churchyard cross. The nave arcades are decorated with unusual carved capitals including a Green Man and a dragon; these are early fourteenth century.

On the outside look up at the north side of the tower where two gargoyles are pulling faces (or 'girning'). The weathervane, which answers to the name 'Cock Peter', may have been made about 1430 and is certainly one of the oldest in England.

Oakham market probably started in the eleventh century around the defended site that evolved into the Norman castle. The Market Cross, also known as the Butter Cross, is a polygonal timber structure supported by a stone pillar and sundial, probably built in the late seventeenth century. The town once had four other crosses but these are now all lost. A set of stocks with five holes is now underneath the Market Cross.

The wool trade made Oakham wealthy in the fourteenth and fifteenth centuries. Flore's House by the pelican crossing on the main road (and now the Tourist Information Centre) is an important example of a late fourteenth century stone hall, with an original door and one hall window; parts of the roof are also original. In the fifteenth century the upper end of the hall was reconstructed and about 1600 a large cross-wing was added. At this time the hall was divided into two floors and fireplaces were inserted. The builder of the first house may have been the local notable William Flore or his son, also William, Speaker of the House of Commons who lived until 1427.

St John's Chapel is the only survival of the medieval hospital. The house known as the Judges' Lodgings is early eighteenth century, as is Haynes House further west.

The Grammar School was founded in 1584 by Archdeacon Johnson (who simultaneously founded **Uppingham** school) and is now a public school. The oldest buildings are to the north-east of All Saints' church. Interestingly there were no additions to the school until the early twentieth century, with major expansion between 1965 and 1982. Older buildings converted for the school's use include the town gaol, the terminal of the canal, hunt stables and lodges, and the early nineteenth century rectory. The school's war memorial chapel has a tympanum carved in 1924–5 by Francis William Sargant, brother of the then headmaster, depicting the risen

Christ and reliefs of dead soldiers being mourned, all in fourteenth century Florentine style.

Our Lady's Well was once famed for curing sore eyes – providing that a pin was thrown in first. In 1291 indulgences could be obtained by visiting Oakham Church during its patronal festival and, for a price, joining a pilgrimage to Our Lady's Well. In 1881 it was visited by the future Queen Alexandra. The well is to the north-east of the town, in a somewhat overgrown area between the **Cottesmore** road and a modern housing estate (141:866095).

The canal, opened in 1803, and the railway, opened in 1848, brought renewed prosperity to the town, accompanied by growth of the school. Many of the older buildings in Oakham were replaced by nineteenth century brick brought in by the railway which arrived in 1850, although the red-and-blue brick houses facing each other in High Street are made from local brick. The predominance of brick-built properties makes Oakham seem more like a 'typical Midlands town' than other settlements in the county, where stone buildings predominate.

Oakham's lesser-known treasures include twelve man-hole covers in the town that bear the name of Thomas Crapper (1837–1910), the pioneer of Victorian sanitation. The signal box near the railway station is doubly famous, at least among boys of a certain age. It was used as an illustration for Hornby model railways and the 'prototype' of an Airfix kit in the 1960s.

The Rutland County Museum contains a wide range of archaeological and historical artefacts, a number of which are mentioned elsewhere in this guide. The building was originally the riding school of the local volunteer cavalry regiment formed in 1794, and was converted to a museum in the late 1960s.

Somerfield's supermarket in the High Street has ceramic relief made in 1984 by Martin Minshall depicting inhabitants and the market place and cross.

Pickworth

130:993138

Pickworth is the only village on an old route (now mostly reduced to a bridleway) from where the Sewstern Lane joins the Great North Road (A1) near **Greetham** to the historically-important crossing of the West Glen River at **Essendine** and the crossing of River Gwash at **Ryhall**. It is also on the road running north from Stamford towards Ancaster.

These routes appears to have been of some strategic importance in the Middle Ages as they are overlooked by two castle earthworks near Pickworth. One is just across the Lincolnshire boundary (130:008143); the other is just inside **Great Casterton** parish, at Woodhead (130:997116). Indeed the '-worth' part of the place name suggests that Pickworth was a locally important, perhaps defended site, in the middle Anglo-Saxon period (such '-worth' place-names tend to be on boundaries, as with Pickworth).

Although now all but deserted, the village was much larger and very prosperous during the reign of Edward II (1327–77). Records reveal that all the inhabitants had gone by 1490; perhaps the buildings were destroyed after the Battle of **Empingham** in 1470. Evidence for lost buildings is revealed by various earthworks around Manor Farm (although some of these 'humps and bumps' are attributable to more recent limestone quarrying), and show that the medieval village had an unusually dispersed arrangement.

The poet John Clare (1793–1864) worked here in 1812 as a lime burner and wrote 'Pickworth is a place of other days... it appears to be the ruins of a large town or city [...] the place where we dug the kiln was full of foundations and human bones.' The lime kiln where Clare worked was cleared out in 1989; access is just to the west of the 30 mph signs on the western edge of the village.

The church, built in the fourteenth century, was ruined by the end of the fifteenth century, presumably at the time the rest of the village was greatly reduced. The spire and tower survived until about 1730, when they were taken down to repair bridges at Wakerley and **Great Casterton**. Several seventeenth century farmhouses probably reuse stone from the church. Near to Manor Farm one arch of this church survives. This may have been re-erected as a folly; although it may be on the site of the medieval church.

The limekiln at Pickworth.

The present parish church of All Saints was built in 1823–4, perhaps on the site of the medieval church, and attempts to copy the eighteenth century rebuilding of **Tickencote**. Inside is a late example of a three-decker pulpit, originally situated at the west end, and some painted box pews.

Pilton

141:915029

Pilton is a small hamlet on the upper reaches of the River Chater. Although stone quarries opened here in 1912, followed later by brickworks, these have all closed.

St Nicholas church is rather small. The building originated in the thirteenth century but seventeenth and nineteenth century restorations were substantial and included rebuilding the chancel in 1852. The typical Rutland double bellcote was probably rebuilt in the nineteenth century.

There is a stone-built dovecote behind Bay House Farm to the south-west of the church.

Pilton church.

One of the more impressive ironstone houses in Preston.

Preston

141:870024

Preston is one of the most attractive villages in the county. The many ironstone houses include several from the seventeenth century, such as the Manor House, schoolhouse and Hall.

The church, dedicated to SS Peter and Paul, has beautifully decorated twelfth century Romanesque arcades. The tower, chancel, south arcade, font, sedile (a sedilia with only one seat) and priest's doorway are fourteenth century. Most of the exterior is fourteenth or fifteenth century. The interior was extensively restored in 1856. There is an alms box with a depiction of St George and the dragon from the Near East, floor tiles from Istanbul and candlesticks from Damascus.

Ridlington

141:847027

Earthworks to the west of the village are probably early Iron Age, and Twitch Hill Farm derives its name from an Anglo-Saxon 'toot hill' or look-out.

The church is mostly thirteenth century. However it had fallen into ruin by the mid-nineteenth century and was rather unsympathetically restored in about 1860. Inside a Romanesque

51

Ridlington tympanum.

tympanum has been incorporated into the west wall of the south aisle. It depicts a lion, a griffin and an eight-spoked wheel. The lettering may say 'John'. There is also an unusual three-sided font, a seventeenth century alabaster effigy depicting James and Frances Harrington (died 1614 and 1599), and a collection of old musical instruments used before the organ.

The village was owned by the Harrington family from 1553 until recent times. The older houses in the village are built from ironstone and have thatched roofs.

Ryhall
130:036108
In the seventh century Ryhall was associated with two women who initially had a reputation as wild hunting girls but later became Christian hermits. Tibba was related to the Mercian king, Penda and her cell was where the church now stands. Tibba's cousin, Eabba, lived nearby. Legend holds that Tibba walked each morning up the hill to wash at a spring which became known as St Tibba's Well. After her death she became the patron saint of falconers and wildfowlers, as a result of her earlier love of hunting. There was an Anglo-Saxon meeting place known as Hale Green, on the brow of Stibbalswell Hill. Gatherings continued there on St Tibba's Day (14th December) until the nineteenth century.

Tibba's cousin gave her name to St Eabba's Well, which in turn gave its name to Stableford (St Eabba's well ford) Bridge over the River Gwash. This well was later known as Shepherd Jacob's Well.

St John the Evangelist's church, on the site of St Tibba's seventh century cell, has a thirteenth century tower and broach spire. The rest of the exterior is mostly fifteenth century and from this date

One of the more intriguing figures from the fifteenth century frieze around Ryhall church.

come the many carved heads on the external frieze, including a foliage-sprouting animal, lots of face-pulling (or 'girning') heads, tongue pokers and what, for want of a better description, might be termed a 'bum poker'. Other figurative carvings include green men, dragons and other mythical animals.

Inside the wide nave is flanked by attractive thirteenth century arcades. Of the same date are the chancel and tower arches. In the chancel is a splendid double sedilia dating from about 1330–40 (although the chancel may have been rebuilt about 1400). Note how the tops of the arches of the sedilia project forwards – these are known to architectural historians as 'nodding ogee arches'. Look out for the wall monument to a vicar's son who died in 1696, aged 2 years 15 days, and the heartfelt eulogy.

The vaulted cellar of the Green Dragon Inn seems to have been part of the thirteenth century manor house. Also to the north of the church is Ryhall Hall, a sixteenth century manor house, enlarged early in the eighteenth century, with a cast-iron balcony added about 1800. There is an attractive stone-built dovecote near the entrance. Although the late twentieth century additions make this one of the less attractive Rutland villages, there are still a number of stone-built houses of the seventeenth and eighteenth centuries. Church Farm nearby has the date of 1685 carved in relief on its chimneystack, following a precedent set by the stack of Old Manor Farm in 1679.

Tolethorpe Hall is to the west of the village – see **Little Casterton**.

Seaton

141:904983

Barrows Farm to the south of the parish takes its name from a line of prehistoric burial mounds on the ridge above the River Welland that continues to **Lyddington**.

An Anglo-Saxon cemetery with both cremations and inhumations has been discovered recently on a hill near Seaton; this is tentatively dated to the early Christian period. A place called Syrepol is recorded in the early fifteenth century. This may be the 'shire pool', the meeting place for Wrangdyke Hundred, the local administration in the Anglo-Saxon era.

The twelfth century foundations of All Hallows church were discovered during the extensive renovations of 1874–5. The south doorway is an excellent example of late Romanesque decoration. Inside, the beautiful chancel arch is also late twelfth century, as is the striking north arcade with alternate bands of limestone and ironstone. The south arcade was built a few decades later. The tower and spire is late thirteenth century. In 1875 the interesting old font was cut up to form a seat. The old parish chest survives, as do the sedilia, piscina and aumbries (unusually with the doors restored). In a recess in the south aisle is an effigy. It may represent Roger de Seaton, who was the Chief Justice of England under Henry III, and died in 1280. The alabaster reredos was erected in 1889.

Seaton from the south.

There are ancient tombstones incorporated into the outer walls. The south porch is approached by an avenue of rather brooding yew trees.

The towering railway viaduct, with 82 arches each 70 feet high, spans the Welland valley into Northamptonshire. At over ¾ mile in length it is Britain's longest brick-built viaduct. It was constructed 1876–8 and contains an estimated 15 million bricks.

South Luffenham

141:941019

South Luffenham developed at a ford over the River Chater, although the part south of the river was only created in 1850 around the first railway junction in Rutland. However the village was on earlier transport routes as a Salter's Cross is recorded in 1615, which alludes to an old salt way.

St Mary's church has a late twelfth century Romanesque north arcade with exceptionally wide arches. The decoration of the capitals is fascinating and includes a hare and various faces, one of which sports a moustache. The south arcade is thirteenth century, while the tower and curiously crocketed spire are fourteenth century; the gargoyles are especially prominent. The chancel is fifteenth century, with a well-preserved fourteenth century effigy of a priest. The 'dug out' medieval parish chest is one of four in Rutland.

The nave is dominated by an ugly round stone pulpit carved in 1861; it has been dubbed the 'parson cooler'. A bell dated 1588 was one of the oldest in the district until it was recast in 1861.

There is a seventeenth century farmhouse near the church. South Luffenham Hall, to the south of the church, is also seventeenth century. A number of interesting small stone-built barns survive amidst the houses, and early eighteenth century stables.

South Luffenham church.

A watermill operated on the River Chater from before Domesday until 1948 (141:945026). The brick tower of a windmill survives (unusually this was built on comparatively low-lying ground), along with the building which housed a steam mill (141:946026).

Stoke Dry

141:856967

Quite how the village acquired its unusual name is uncertain. Stoke is a fairly common place-name and there was a now forgotten Stoke in nearby **Caldecott** parish which would have caused confusion. The 'Dry' affix could either be because it was just above the then-marshy Eye Brook vallet, or because local wells and springs were unreliable.

Part of one of the Romanesque columns in Stoke Dry church.

St Andrew's church has much of interest. The chantry chapel (now used as the vestry) is probably the oldest part of the church, although much transformed over the centuries. There is a 'squint' or hagioscope, enabling people in the chapel to see the main altar.

There is a Romanesque string course in the chancel with tendrils, animals and humans. The chancel arch columns and the surviving capital are decorated with deeply-carved figures (a similar style of decoration can also be seen at **Essendine**). They are among the most interesting carvings of this period in the region. Look out for a mermaid, a dragon and one of the earliest depictions of a bell ringer. They are tentatively to about 1120.

The rather slim base to the tower is thirteenth century. It was probably designed to support a typical Rutland bellcote. However the belfry was added in the seventeenth century. It supports a single bell dated 1761.

The south aisle is also thirteenth century. The east window of the south chapel dates from about 1300 and has unusual decoration; the east window of the chancel is the same age. The north aisle is fourteenth century and the clerestory was added in the late fifteenth or early sixteenth century. The north porch with the priest's chamber above is sixteenth century, the south porch dates from the following century.

There is an aumbry in the east wall of the chancel, a piscina in the south wall of the chancel (obscured by the Digby monument), another piscina in the south wall of the chantry chapel, and a stoup in the west wall of the same chapel.

The rather decaying chancel screen is fifteenth century; it seems have been brought from elsewhere and adapted to fit. Most unusually at the top there is ribbed coving which would have originally blended into a rood loft above. Note the north and south doors, made of chamfered oak planks, with the stone steps cut to an exact fit.

A wall painting of St Edmund being martyred by heathen Vikings (who are the spitting image of 'Red Indians') is dated by some to the thirteenth or fourteenth centuries. As the chapel was refurbished in 1574, when woodcuts of native Americans had circulated widely leading to 'Red Indians' epitomising 'heathens' at this time, there is the possibility that this wall painting is partially or entirely sixteenth century (wall paintings elsewhere in the church are more certainly sixteenth century). If the painting of St Edmund is unquestionably much older than the discovery of the New World then it opens up some intriguing thoughts about what sort of people in the fourteenth century dressed up in feather head-dresses and were considered heathens.

The nearby depiction of the Virgin and Child is more probably fourteenth century, and one of the best-surviving wall paintings of this date in the region. Elsewhere in the church are sixteenth century depictions of the emblems of the Twelve Tribes of Israel. All the wall paintings were revealed during restoration work in 1898, when the roofs were extensively repaired while still retaining as many old timbers as possible.

There are four sepulchral monuments. The oldest is an incised alabaster slab which depicts Jaquetta Digby, who died in 1496. The other effigies commemorate Everard Digby (died 1540), and Kenelme Digby (died 1590), with his wife (who died in 1602), and their eleven children (two of whom died as infants).

The reservoir in the Eye Brook valley was constructed in 1935 to supply Corby steelworks; it now attracts water fowl and ornithologists.

Stretton

130:949157

The place-name is a common one for villages on Roman roads – it is the *tun* [pronounced 'toon' and the origin of the modern word 'town'] on a *straet* or Roman road.

St Nicholas church has a Romanesque doorway with the tympanum made from a 'recycled' Anglo-Saxon coffin lid. The north arcade is early thirteenth century. Most of the rest of the building is sixteenth or seventeenth century, extensively but sensitively restored in 1881–2. Access to the church is along a lane opposite the inn in the village.

The Ram Jam Inn on the A1 is always regarded as being in Stretton, although technically it is in **Greetham** parish. It takes its name from a potent drink served to refresh travellers in the days of horse-drawn coaches, although various dubious tales purport to offer alternative explanations of the name.

Despite the dominance of the A1 some pleasant old farm buildings survive. The early seventeenth century Stocken Hall (altered about 1774 and in 1876–7) is now part of a prison farm.

So close to the A1 but seldom seen – Stretton's secluded church.

Teigh

130:865160

The village name is pronounced 'Tee'; the name originally denoted a small enclosure.

Three medieval fishponds and other earthworks, probably of a manor house complex, survive to the west of the village. Intriguingly, the road loops in a semi-circle around the churchyard.

Holy Trinity church was rebuilt in the eighteenth century and retains its interior furnishings, making it unique in Rutland (although there are close parallels with Stapleford church just four miles away in Leicestershire, as both were rebuilt by the same patron and architect).

Only the tower survives from the medieval building; the lower part is thirteenth century and the upper part fourteenth century. The rest was rebuilt in 1782. The furnishings inside have survived from this date, making it one of the few to have survived the ravages of Victorian Gothic revivalism (although tracery was inserted into the windows between 1892–5). The west end is dominated by a curious pulpit (no less than thirteen feet above ground), flanked by a pair of reading desks. Behind is a painted landscape as if seen through a window. The pews face each other, an arrangement known as 'collegiate style'. The font was carved in 1845 by the rector.

Teigh church.

Thistleton

130:913180

The village name is what it seems – a farm or settlement renowned for its thistles. Thistles grow best on disturbed ground and old settlements. As the village presumably acquired its name in early Anglo-Saxon times, this could refer to thistles growing on old Romano-British settlements. Just such a site, a Roman villa, was discovered in 1956 about half a mile south of St Nicholas' church.

Thistleton church.

However far more substantial Roman remains are known from the ironstone quarries towards Market Overton. A substantial Iron Age settlement developed, based around iron working. There was a shrine near the centre. The town may have had trading links to the east as a number of Iron Age coins were found here (coins are typically found at late Iron Age towns in Lincolnshire, but not at those in Leicestershire). The Romans continued to work iron here and a small town developed; the Iron Age shrine developed into a Roman temple. A probable Roman road runs from the Fosse Way (modern A46) at Syston in Leicestershire, north-east along a ridge towards Frisby on the Wreak, where it turns east towards Thistleton.

Probably the iron working made Thistleton into an important 'sub-regional' centre in the Iron Age, throughout the Roman era, and into the Anglo-Saxon period.

St Nicholas church has a fourteenth century tower although the rest was rebuilt in 1879–80.

Tickencote

141:990095

The meaning of the place-name suggests a rather mundane origin – there was once nothing more distinctive hereabouts than 'a shed for young goats'.

SS Peter and Paul's church is perhaps best described as 'Normanesque'. The nave was restored in 1792 by Samuel Pepys

Cockerell who had earlier in his career been Clerk of Works at the Tower of London, where the White Tower is a fine example of Norman architecture. However in the eighteenth century Norman (Romanesque) architecture was not fully understood and the west front is a unique blend of eleventh and eighteenth century ideas.

The stone vaulted roof of the chancel is unique in an English parish church and comparable only to the choir of Canterbury Cathedral (which was built later in the twelfth century). At the apex is a boss carved with three faces, said to depict a monk's head and two muzzled bears. It is probably the oldest Romanesque roof boss in the country.

The impressive eighteenth century mill building at Tickencote.

Above the chancel is a priest's chamber, although the stairs providing access were removed in 1792. Such priest's chambers above chancels have rarely survived.

The chancel arch is a *tour de force* of Romanesque exuberance. There are seven bands of decoration, including squared-off foliage and menacing beak heads. It was probably built between 1130–50 and the craftsmen may have been the same ones responsible for the west front of the church at Tutbury, Staffordshire. It should have been semi-circular but poor construction has caused it to 'slump'.

In the nave are twelve deeply-carved twelfth century corbels; they include a green man, two tongue pokers, and one who is face-pulling or 'girning'. The nave roof was renewed in 1875. At the same time the previously plain doorways from the nave to the vestry and to the porch were made to look Romanesque.

The rather wonderful font dates from about 1200. The main decoration comprises architectural arcades and stylised vegetation, but there are human heads on the corners. The columns on the base were carved into a previously plain stone sometime after 1820.

In a recess in the chancel is an over life-size oak effigy of a thirteenth century knight. The present altar stands on a slab of Purbeck marble that is probably the pre-Reformation altar.

Tickencote has literary connections as the eighteenth century poet John Clare (1793–1864) met his wife, Martha ('Sweet Patty of the Vale'). while drinking at the Flower Pot Inn (now a house) in Tickencote.

There is an old mill by the River Gwash to the south-west of the church; it stopped working in the 1900s. The impressive stone-built building is eighteenth century.

Tinwell
141:006063

All Saints church has a massive tower of the thirteenth or fourteenth century with the only saddleback roof in Rutland. The nave arcade and chancel arch are thirteenth century, and the chancel dates from the fifteenth century. There is a monument to the sister of the first Lord Burghley; she died in 1611. Look out for the charming seventeenth century warning to illicit bell ringers under the tower.

The village is famous for the forge, built in 1848, with a horseshoe-shaped doorway. It later became the Post Office but has now been reclaimed as a forge. The building next door was the bakery until the 1920s.

Tinwell Forge.

The eleventh century tower arch inside Tixover church.

Tixover

141:971998

Aspects of Tixover's prehistory have been tantalisingly revealed by aerial photography. There is evidence for Bronze Age burial mounds, now ploughed away, and for Bronze Age or Iron Age 'triple ditches' which are probably associated with territorial boundaries. The Romans were here too, as the base of a timber bridge and the remains of a mosaic pavement (suggesting a villa site) were found to the south of the St Mary Magdalene's church. A second Roman villa is known on the north side of the A47.

The medieval village was nearer to the main road, as extensive 'humps and bumps' can be seen between the A47 and the present village. Among the many attractive and interesting buildings in the small village is a dovecote in the grounds of Manor Farm that may be eighteenth century.

St Mary Magdalen's church is on the north shore of the River Welland, remote from the village along an unmade track. Several early stone coffin lids are now in the churchyard. The oldest part of the structure is the main part of the tower, which is early twelfth century (making it one of the three oldest towers in the country), topped with a fifteenth century parapet. Look out for the interesting gargoyle on the east side of the tower, which *may* be early twelfth century too. There is a later twelfth century south doorway and south arcade, and an early thirteenth century north arcade (unusually the south arcade is earlier than the north arcade). The chancel is also thirteenth century.

Inside there is an eleventh century tower arch (see photograph on previous page) and font (apparently mutilated at some later date), original medieval stone seats along the wall of the chancel, along with an aumbry, piscina and sedilia, and ancient glass (mostly imported from Europe) in a south aisle window. Behind the piscina is a stone carved with a geometrical design which was probably a late Saxon or early Norman grave marker. The 'poppy head' ends to the pews are seventeenth century. There is a curious corbel depicting a draped figure supporting the arch at the west end of the north arcade. Interestingly, this church is one of the few in Rutland that appears not to have been restored in any way during the nineteenth century.

Uppingham

141:866996

The market charter for Uppingham was granted in 1281. The continuing wealth this brought to the town is revealed by the variety of high quality inns and houses in the High Street which date from the late sixteenth century to the early nineteenth century.

The church of SS Peter and Paul is usually approached via a short 'walkway' which makes the south porch of the church almost part of the market place. However the church sits above a steep slope to the south, with the churchyard flowing down the hillside.

Inside there are four Romanesque half-figures in the south entrance and north aisle east window. These were carved about 1200 and include a depiction of a bearded saint blessing and of Christ blessing. The north aisle, decorated with heads, is thirteenth or fourteenth century. The tower and imposing spire are fourteenth century. The whole church was drastically restored in 1861, although the sixteenth century pulpit was retained.

Uppingham School was founded in 1584 by Archdeacon Johnson. The original building survives near the south side of the parish church. It remained of local importance only until the appointment of Rev Edward Thring as headmaster in 1853 (a fine seated life-size sculpture of Thring occupies the north-east porch of the school's chapel). The school then grew rapidly and now plays a major part in the town's economy. Numerous existing buildings were adapted and extended for the school's use. Purpose-built buildings include the Arts and Crafts-inspired thatched cricket pavilion on Seaton Road, and the rather Alpine-looking buttery and music centre, built about 1980.

The town is home to Rutland's oldest Methodist chapel (dated 1814) by the traffic lights (the only set in Rutland!).

Uppingham Methodist chapel.

Wardley

141:832003

The few houses of the village straddle a steep hill with good views across the Eye valley to the west. This probably accounts for the village's name, which means 'look out clearing'.

The Normans built a small castle on the parish boundary with **Uppingham** (141:850005). The defences skilfully incorporate the natural protection of a triangular promontory, although the outer bailey has been ploughed away. As the location has no strategic importance it was probably the residence of a royal forester responsible for the area used for hunting known as Beaumont Chase (a second forester

Wardley church.

was based at **Braunston**). However preliminary archaeological investigation revealed evidence for considerable iron working; such a combination of forest administration and iron working was associated with the Norman castle at Hallaton, Leicestershire.

St Botolph's church also has Norman origins, with a south doorway dating from about 1175 and a north doorway of about 1200. The church was thoroughly restored in 1861 and the chancel was rebuilt in 1871. Inside there is a late eighteenth century font, Commandment boards, a small barrel organ and early nineteenth century pews that have lost their doors.

Whissendine

130:833143

The present village is rather scattered, with new estates built in the 1970s. The oldest-known settlement site survives as a well-preserved moat on Moor Lane (130:838151). This is believed to be the site of the manor of Moorhall, mentioned in 1306. There is another moat

A fabulous 'girning' roof boss carved in 1728.
Whissendine church.

nearby. One of the oldest surviving buildings is the seventeenth century Manor House to the east of St Andrew's church.

Whissendine has one of the largest parish churches in the county. The arcades are thirteenth or fourteenth century. The tower is fourteenth century. The aisle windows and clerestory date from the fifteenth century.

The attractive interior is mostly thirteenth century. There are excellent stone corbels and faces decorating the arches. Indeed, there is a wonderful collection of wooden and stone figurative carving. Look out for the heads among the stylised leaf decoration in the north aisle arcade. The roof is fifteenth century but was extensively restored in 1728. There are decorated bosses, including one 'face puller', and elaborate corbels comprising double figures (the lower figures probably fifteenth century and supporting larger figures of 1728). The font is fourteenth century. The sixteenth century south aisle screen was originally in St John's College, Cambridge. The interior was subject to extensive restorations 1864–70.

A restored seven-storey windmill stands outside the village (130:823143); associated buildings include something that is still a rarity in Rutland – a tea shop.

Whitwell
141:924087
Evidence for Iron Age and Roman settlement has been found between the village and the shore of Rutland Water. The humps and bumps of the medieval village, to the south of the church, have been partly excavated by local archaeologists.

St Michael's church with its double bellcote, is rather small and now sits perched above a retaining wall on top of a hill. One corner of the nave may be a survival from an Anglo-Saxon church. The bellcote is thirteenth century and probably the oldest in Rutland. The decoration on the font, with a wheel and other shapes, dates from about 1200, although it may be an eleventh century font partly 'recut' but leaving some of the original foliate decoration. There are no less than four piscinas and also a squint. Among the unexciting Victorian glass introduced during the restoration of 1881 try to locate the fourteenth century stained glass depicting the Crucifixion. There are old wooden figures of St Michael and the Archangel Gabriel.

There are two aspects of this church which are unusual and not readily recognised. The first is that a stream flows underneath the chancel from a spring higher up the slope. The second is that the

The curiously situated church at Whitwell.

church is not aligned exactly east-west and is the only church in Rutland which aligns with sunrise on the feast day of its patron saint (allowing for the fact that sunrise is delayed by an intervening hill). The alignment of the church, if extended, points directly towards All Saint's church, **Oakham** in the west and **Great Casterton** church in the east.

Wing

141:894029

Unusually for Rutland the place-name is not Anglo-Saxon but Anglo-Scandinavian for 'field', suggesting that there was no settlement here before about the ninth century. The main part of the village comprises stone-built houses dating from the sixteenth to eighteenth centuries. There have been few changes since the 1880s.

The village is best-known for its turf labyrinth or maze, now surrounded by a wooden fence, on the roadside at the south-east of the village (141:896028). Only eight such turf mazes have survived in Britain, although many now-lost examples have been documented (including one on Priestly Hill near **Lyddington**; 141:883973). The Wing maze has the same design as a tile labyrinth on the floor of Chartres Cathedral, and another British turf maze at Alkborough in

Wing maze.

Yorkshire. The first documented reference to the Wing labyrinth is in 1631 although it is reasonable to suppose that these turf mazes originate in the medieval era. Given the need for regular maintenance and recutting, the survival of turf labyrinths for so many centuries is quite remarkable.

The church of SS Peter and Paul has a south arcade built about 1150. The north arcade and a chancel arch (decorated with heads) is later twelfth century. Also Romanesque is the doorway inside a porch built as part of the restorations of 1875 (when the chancel was rebuilt) and 1885.

Bibliography of sources

Victoria County History: Rutland part 1 (1908) and part 2 (1935).

Barber, John L., 1984, 'Thomas Crapper and manhole covers', *Rutland Record*, 4, 152–3.

Billson, Charles J., 1895, *Leicestershire and Rutland: County Folklore*, Folklore Society.

Blore, T., 1811, *The History and Antiquities of the County of Rutland.*

Bourne, Jill, 1981, *Place-names of Leicestershire and Rutland* (2nd edn), Leicestershire Libraries.

Brandwood, Geoffrey K., 2002, *Bringing Them to Their Knees: Church building and restoration in Leicestershire and Rutland 1800–1914*, Leicestershire Archaeological and Historical Society.

Brown, Mike, 1999, *Tiger Tales and Ales: A Directory of Leicestershire Brewers (including Rutland) 1400–1999*, Brewery History Society.

Cantor, L.M., 1976–7, 'The medieval parks of Leicestershire, part 2, *Transactions of Leicestershire Archaeological and Historical Society*, 52, 73–6.

Cantor, L.M., 1980, 'The medieval hunting grounds of Rutland', *Rutland Record*, 1, 13–18.

Cantor, Leonard, 1998, *The Historic Country Houses of Leicestershire and Rutland*, Kairos Press.

Cavanagh, Terry and Alison Yarrington, 2000, *Public Sculpture of Leicestershire and Rutland*, Liverpool University Press.

Clough, T.H.McK., Ann Dornier and R.A. Rutland, 1975, *Anglo-Saxon and Viking Leicestershire including Rutland*, Leicestershire Museums.

Cooper, Nicholas J., 2000, *The Archaeology of Rutland Water*, University of Leicester Archaeological Services.

Cox, Barrie, 1990, 'Rutland in the Danelaw: A field-names perspective', *Journal of the English Place-name Society*, 22, 7–22.

Cox, Barrie, 1994, *The Place-names of Rutland*, English Place-name Society.

Creighton, Oliver, 1999, 'Early castles in the medieval landscape of Rutland' in *Transactions of the Leicestershire Archaeological and Historical Society* Vol.73 pp19–33.

Davies, Richard, 1984, 'Church orientation in Rutland', *Rutland Record*, 4, 142–3.

Dickinson, Gillian (ed.), 1983, *Rutland Churches before Restoration*, Barrowden Books. [This includes illustrations prepared in 1838–9 of all the county's churches.]

Dickinson, Gillian, 1984, *Rutland: A guide and gazetteer*, Barrowden Books.

Hartley, Robert F., 1983, *The Medieval Earthworks of Rutland: A survey*, Leicestershire Museums.

Hopewell, Jeffery, 1989, *Leicestershire and Rutland*, Shire Publications.

Hoskins, W.G., 1949, *Rutland*, City of Leicester Publicity Dept.

Hoskins, W.G., 1963, *Shell Guide to Rutland*, Faber.

Lee, Joyce and Jon Dean, 1995, *Curiosities of Leicestershire and Rutland*, S.B. Publications.

Lee, Michael, 1993, 'A turret clock at St Mary's Edith Weston', *Rutland Record*, 13, 129–35.

Liddle, Peter, 1983, *A Guide to Twenty Sites in Leicestershire*, Leicestershire Museums.

Liddle, Peter, 1995, 'Roman small towns in Leicestershire', in A.E. Brown (ed), *Roman Small Towns in Eastern England and Beyond*, Oxbow.

Lott, Graham, 2001, 'Geology and building stones in the East Midlands', *Mercian Geologist*, 15 (2), 97–122.

Matthews, Bryan, 1978, *The Book of Rutland*, Barracuda Books.

Matthews, Max, 2002, *Sepulchral Effigies in Leicestershire and Rutland*, Heart of Albion Press.

Meadows, Ian, 1999, 'Ketton Quarry', *Transactions of the Leicestershire Archaeological and Historical Society*, 73, 119–23.

Ovens, Robert and Sheila Sleath, 2002, *Time in Rutland: A History and Gazetteer of the Bells, Clocks and Sundials of Rutland*, Rutland Local History and Record Society.

Palmer, Marilyn and Peter Neaverson, 1991, 'Industrial archaeology in Rutland', *Rutland Record*, 11, 18–24.

Palmer, Roy, 1985, *The Folklore of Leicestershire and Rutland*, Sycamore Press.

Pevsner, Nikolaus (revised by E. Williamson and G. Brandwood), 1984, *Leicestershire and Rutland* (The Buildings of England series), 2nd edn (reprinted with corrections 1998), Penguin.

Phythian-Adams, Charles, 1977, 'Rutland reconsidered' in Ann Dornier (ed), *Mercian Studies*, Leicester University Press.

Phythian-Adams, Charles, 1980, 'The emergence of Rutland and the making of the realm', *Rutland Record*, 1, 5–12.

Phythian-Adams, Charles (ed), 1986, *The Norman Conquest of Leicestershire and Rutland*, Leicestershire Museums.

Sharpling, Paul, 1997, *Stained Glass in Rutland Churches*, Rutland Local History and Record Society.

Squires, Anthony and Michael Jeeves, 1994, *Leicestershire and Rutland Woodlands Past and Present*, Kairos Press.

Thomas, John and Roger Jacobi, 2001, 'Glaston', *Current Archaeology*, No.173, 180–4.

Thorn, Frank (ed.), 1980, *Domesday Book: Rutland*, Phillimore.

Timby, Jane, 1996, *The Anglo-Saxon Cemetery at Empingham II, Rutland*, Oxbow Books.

Trubshaw, Bob, 1994, 'Goddess or queen? The enigmatic carving at Braunston in Rutland', *Mercian Mysteries*, 21, 4–5.

Trubshaw, Bob, 1995, *Little-known Leicestershire and Rutland*, Heart of Albion Press.

Trubshaw, Bob, 2002, *Interactive Little-known Leicestershire and Rutland*, Heart of Albion Press.

Waites, Brian, 1982, *Exploring Rutland*, Leicester Libraries.

Whitelaw, Jeffery W., 1996, *Hidden Leicestershire and Rutland*, Countryside Books.

Wright, James, 1684, *History and Antiquities of the County of Rutland*.

Also numerous church guide leaflets, mostly anonymous.

Also published by Heart of Albion Press

Explore Mythology

Bob Trubshaw

Myths are usually thought of as something to do with 'traditional cultures'. The study of such 'traditional' myths emphasises their importance in religion, national identity, hero-figures, understanding the origin of the universe, and predictions of an apocalyptic demise. The academic study of myths has done much to fit these ideas into the preconceived ideas of the relevant academics.

Only in recent years have such long-standing assumptions about myths begun to be questioned, opening up whole new ways of thinking about the way such myths define and structure how a society thinks about itself and the 'real world'.

196 pages, 4 line drawings, paperback **£9.95** plus 80p p&p.

Explore Folklore

Bob Trubshaw

There have been fascinating developments in the study of folklore in the last twenty-or-so years, but few books about British folklore and folk customs reflect these exciting new approaches. As a result there is a huge gap between scholarly approaches to folklore studies and 'popular beliefs' about the character and history of British folklore. *Explore Folklore* is the first book to bridge that gap, and to show how much 'folklore' there is in modern day Britain.

196 pages, 4 line drawings, paperback **£9.95** plus 80p p&p.

Further details of all Heart of Albion titles online at
www.hoap.co.uk

Also published by Heart of Albion Press

*Interactive
Little-known
Leicestershire
and Rutland*

Text and photographs
by Bob Trubshaw

For seventeen years the author has been researching the 'little-known' aspects of Leicestershire and Rutland. Topics include holy wells, standing stones and mark stones, medieval crosses, and a wide variety of Romanesque and medieval figurative carvings - and a healthy quota of 'miscellaneous' sites.

Some of this information appeared in early Heart of Albion publications (mostly long out of print), but this CD-ROM contains extensive further research. The information covers 241 parishes and includes no less than 550 'large format' colour photographs (all previously unpublished).

There are introductory essays, a glossary and plenty of hypertext indexes.

Runs on PCs and Macs.

ISBN 1 872883 53 2
£14.95 incl. VAT.

Special offer!

Mail order customers save 17.5% (because Heart of Albion is not VAT registered) = **£12.70** plus 80p p&p.

Also published by Heart of Albion Press

Sepulchral Effigies in Leicestershire and Rutland

Text by Max Wade Matthews

Photographs by Bob Trubshaw

This CD-ROM makes available for the first time details of the wealth of sepulchral effigies in Leicestershire and Rutland - from thirteenth century priests, thorough alabaster knights in armour and their ladies, to the splendours of seventeenth century Classical aggrandisement. There are even a number of twentieth century effigies too.

350 photos depict 141 effigies in 72 churches, all with detailed descriptions and useful hypertext indexes. Runs on PCs and Macs.

ISBN 1 872883 54 0 **£14.95** incl. VAT.

Special offer!

Mail order customers save 17.5% (because Heart of Albion is not VAT registered) = **£12.70** plus 80p p&p.

Also available from Heart of Albion Press

A Walk Round Leicester

Max Wade Matthews

See Leicester like never before! Over 1,300 stunning photographs and many sound clips take the 'walker' through over 2,000 years of history from a Roman milestone to the twenty-first century National Space Museum.

Available from Heart of Albion Press for **£14.95** incl. VAT.

Special offer!

Mail order customers save 17.5% (because Heart of Albion is not VAT registered) = **£12.70** plus 80p p&p.

Also available from Heart of Albion Press

The History and Antiquities
of the County of Rutland

James Wright

First published in 1684, this pioneering work on local history
contains a wealth of information. However copies of the book are
hard to come by, so the entire text has been scanned in and made
available as high resolution images on this CD-ROM.

Available from Heart of Albion Press for **£10.00** plus 80p p&p

Full details of current Heart of Albion
publications online at www.hoap.co.uk

To order books or request our current catalogue please contact

Heart of Albion Press

2 Cross Hill Close, Wymeswold
Loughborough, LE12 6UJ

Phone: 01509 880725
Fax: 01509 881715
email: albion@indigogroup.co.uk
Web site: www.hoap.co.uk

Totally FREE Community Advertising

Rutland on the.net

The Premier Resource Finder and Community based website for Rutland!

Search for sports, restaurants, museums and many more local services & activities. Have your say by placing articles and information about Rutland.

Advertise your local charity events, fetes, galas etc. Why not post your local pub sports fixtures & results. Are you a member of a group or society? Keep in touch on the net, send in your news and views!

Reach your target audience in Rutland, quickly and easily by posting your events, stories, news and views!

To search or advertise local companies, to keep in touch and share stories just visit;

www.rutlandonthe.net